I THOUGH I WAS DONE WITH THIS

MAURICE HOFMANN

Copyright © 2021 by Maurice Hofmann. All rights reserved.

No part of this publication may be reproduced, stored in a retrieval system or transmitted in any way by any means, electronic, mechanical, photocopy, recording or otherwise without the prior permission of the author except as provided by USA copyright law.

Contents

Acknowledgments 5

Foreword 7

Every Damn Day..15

Am I my Brother's Keeper? 17

Fighting Back 22

My Responsibility or My Fights, My fault 25

Bigger City, Bigger Minds...28

Clean the Mind 29

Education and Perspective..31

Rumble and Tumble of Black Teenagers in Germany 33

German Army 38

Black-Owned Agency 42

German Hip-Hop History – How I Met U.S. Rap Legends....44

The Hard Way – MBA...51

Welcome to the U.S.A...53

Racism – I Thought I was Done with This.............................57

Understanding and Capturing Racism in the USA...................67

Change Must Come from Within 69

Holistic Programs Focused on More
Than Just Education & Perspectives 72

Change of Mindset...75

How I Turned it Around for Myself...78

Guide: What Can You, I, We All Do?......................................85

Keep breathing...86

Learn Why U.S. Police Officers Have
More in Common with Soldiers in
Afghanistan than Cops in England...88

What Does FUBU Have to do with Politics? 91

Nobody Ever Said Voting was Easy 93

Refocus the Narrative!..98

Everyday Skills as a Basis for Further Education 100

Role Models and Mentorships 102

Master "Whiteface" While Keeping Your Black Identity 103

Colin Kaepernick, the Flag, and What It Tells You................106

White Fragility, or How to Help Them Join the Fight 111

Resources...115

References 121

Acknowledgments

To my mum, Monika.

You showed me how to throw a punch. You told me that black is beautiful, that I am beautiful. You encouraged me to push further while not dictating the direction. You managed to send me to a private school when there was no reason that this was even possible for me.

You had 99 problems, but I felt none.

You were always there for me and still are whenever I need you. There are not enough words to describe what you mean to me.

So just take this: I am proud of you, and I love you.

To my son, Marvin Jackson.

Your existence is all I needed to strive to become the best version of me because I want to be a father you can feel proud of. You made me explore my roots and find our family. You motivate me to fight for this world to become a better place.

You are the reason this book exists.

You, the robots you build, and the stories you tell me are the highlights of my every day. You give the best and strongest hugs ever.

Because of you, I have the best title anyone could ever archive, daddy.

Your daddy.
I love you more than you will ever know.

To: Brent, Chris, Christophe, Dee, Dia, Lawrence, Lucienne, Marco, Mola, Providence, Sascha, Shawn, Shay, Sebastiao, Terrence, Tony, Tyron

One Love!

Maurice with son Marvin in front of "Spike's Joint", Brooklyn, NY; July 2020

FOREWORD

I thought I was done with this.

I thought I was done with racism.

I was honestly done with it. I felt no limitations, nor did I think I had to discuss racism all the time or even think about it very often. I had paid my dues and fought my fights – I have the scars to prove it. I was truly and utterly done.

Or so I thought.

But here we are again; racism is everywhere. It feels so 1960s, over 60 years later, in 2021. And here I thought racism was something I had left behind in Germany in the 1980s.

Talking about race is difficult anywhere globally; the topic is complicated, and there is more than one reason we're talking about it again. The need to discuss racism is incredibly real in the United States of America, where I moved from Germany in 2010. That move reintroduced to me the omnipresent racism I had forgotten.

The truth is, the human species doesn't feature multiple races. The differences between Europeans, Asians, Blacks, Native Americans, and others are too insignificant to qualify as different races based on science and biology.

But science has become a politicized topic that is less about facts these days and more about beliefs and interpretations, which is, oddly enough, unscientific.

That subject is a great topic for someone else; however, I will stick with science for a moment and discuss Templeton's quote on the biological basis for race. Let's review and digest the concept, and I'll try not to harp on it for the remainder of the book.

> *"Races may exist in humans in a cultural sense, but biological concepts of race are needed to access their reality in a non-species-specific manner and to see if cultural categories correspond to biological categories within humans.[…] Adaptive traits, such as skin color, have frequently been used to define races in humans. Still, such adaptive traits reflect the underlying environmental factor to which they are adaptive and not overall genetic differentiation."*
> Alan R. Templeton, *"Biological Races in Humans"*

In short, this means: **There are no races in the human species**. Racism is flawed at its core. If there are no races differentiating humans, then the questions we must ask are, "What is racism all about? What are its merits?" The quick answer: "**Nothing and none.**"

That scientific fact is a bit of a bummer for both racists and racism's victims.

The differences in humans are behavioral, external influences too superficial to qualify as evidence of race. Races only exist in a cultural context and even then are not clearly defined. I suggest you read Mr. Templeton's article published in the U.S. National Library of Medicine and National Institutes of Health – sure, it's not Wikipedia, but still pretty reliable.

Now that we've got that pesky science/fact-based stuff out of the way, we can look at the (cultural) race discussion in the United States. But, instead of mulling over the history of racism, slavery, and police brutality of the past four hundred plus years, I'll focus on what we *can* do to step out of this unforsaken situation.

Since I am originally from Germany (I moved to the U.S. eleven years ago), I wondered whether I should write this book in the first place, cautious about how I would approach the topic. I considered if people would accept my position and suggestions; would I unintentionally poke my finger in the wounds of racism or alienate my brothers and sisters?

When I started writing this book, I researched a ton to validate my position and make sure I am not crazy.

> *Disclaimer: I am nuts, but it is nothing*
> *a doctor can fix, so let's move on.*

During my ten years in the U.S., I repeatedly asked myself why we Black people cannot move beyond racism. Why are we still victims of this awful situation? Is there anything we should be doing? Are we missing something? Are we strong enough to pull ourselves out of this, or do we need outside help?

> *These questions may have already made you angry. That is good. Keep that anger, but put a pin in it for now. We'll need that energy later.*

Let's get back to my research and what experts are saying that you should know.

First off, Morgan Freeman does not believe race has anything to do with wealth distribution in America today. He said race is "like religion to me. It's a good excuse not to get there." During Don Lemon's interview with Mr. Freeman for CNN, Lemon elaborated and said he is tired of talking about racism every day: "This is over. Can we move on?"

I found other statements from people like David Webb, who claimed systemic racism would require a social contract or law; neither exists in the U.S. today. A different personality, Lil Wayne, said he has never dealt with racism in his life and admits he is blessed.

Are we all wrong? Is there no racism in the U.S.? Are we making this up? Are you? Am I?

The statements above are taken out of context and a harsh simplification of the situation. However, they are a good starting point for the discussion I want to have with you. Racism is a discussion we need to have with our children, parents, grandparents, siblings, aunts, uncles, friends, colleagues, and the people from our congregations. This discussion needs to take place with every Black or Brown person with whom you interact. That includes me.

Why do we allow racism to occur? Why do we let racism have such power over us?

David Webb said that how we get to solutions matters and that too many issues plague Blacks in America to quickly address them. Webb challenges us to look at the root cause of our communities' problems. Like Denzel Washington, he points to us, the parents responsible for raising their children. Washington paints a cruel picture, saying that we should not blame the system for Black incarcerations but that the responsibility for this starts in the home: "By the time the system comes into play, the damage is done. They are not locking up seven-year-olds." Washington talked about his childhood and that of his friends, saying they all did foolish things when they were seven – actions that could have landed them in prison. The only difference between Denzel Washington and his three friends who did years, if not decades of prison time, was his parents. Although his mother and father had separated, they called him to order and guided him in the right direction. His three friends lacked this kind of guidance.

Webb said it is easy to make excuses, to argue the emotions of the situation, misapply facts, or speak to narratives. But is it that easy?

Is it just a question of providing our kids with something that at least resembles a stable home? Of making sure both parents are available? How do we break the cycle of record-levels of incarcerated men? How do we get good fathers to stay and protect our sons from becoming another statistic?

That is the prize question: How do we break the cycle?

I'm from Europe, and my experience there taught me that there *is* a way to overcome racism. You can work hard and end up with a closer life to people like Morgan Freeman, Denzel

Washington, or Lil Wayne. Or me. I am not a star, but I do all right. I have a well-paid job that earns me three to four times that of America's average Black family. Is this because of my privileged upbringing? No. It was because my mum played a critical role, and I had a "village" to help raise me and who showed up at crucial intersections.

We must take responsibility to raise our youth and challenge them to make the right turns when they come to key intersections. We must emphasize education. No, more than emphasize – we must drill knowledge into our kids. Nothing can replace education other than more of it and better qualifications.

I wrote this book to look at where we, Black people, are today and explain how we have to stop allowing racism to keep us from achieving our full potential. Racism is not about the racists around us; it is about us and our behavior.

Anthony Mackie put it nicely when he said, "When you are diving in the sea in shark-infested waters, everything around you is considered a threat until proven otherwise. Even if it looks like a guppy, it could be a shark until you know it's a guppy." Mackie said it is time for Blacks to sit down with our young men and women and talk to them about perceptions and stereotypes. As I learned in Germany, young men in the United States must learn to navigate the shark-infested waters surrounding them. Blacks in America must study behavior and learn how to behave to survive. "Yes, officer. No officer. Are we done, officer?" No flailing our hands and crying wolf. We already know sharks are after us; don't complain about it – do something!

Turn that anger you may feel right now into energy to be a change agent. We can't teach the sharks to hunt different food, but we can stop acting like the best, bloody prey in the water.

Before you continue reading, let me give you a hint on what to expect from this book.

If you are looking for a book that pins the blame on the racists and tells white people they need to check themselves, then this is not the book for you.

However, if you are looking for self-empowerment and solutions that originate from within us and are for us, the Black community, continue reading. Then have these types of discussions with your family, friends, and colleagues. You can call me every nasty name under the sun, but please, do not stop having the debate I hope to spark.

Now, let me start at the beginning – my beginning.

EVERY DAMN DAY

It was a typical day during my first few years of school in the small German town, Trier, in western Germany. I looked different than the other German kids named Markus, Tobias, and Ralf. Thanks to my parents, I was what we later described as Afro-German – but not in the 1970s or early eighties, and indeed not that day. They called me Neger (nigger in German) and all kinds of other names. It didn't matter which name they chose that day – I knew there would be a fight on my short way from elementary school to my kindergarten.

How did I know there would be a fight? Because there always was. I got in a row at least three or four times a week, so I knew what was going to happen. The only thing yet to be determined was who I'd fight this time and where it would happen. And along those three hundred yards, there were not too many options. Sure, those little suckers would eventually get in a punch that might sting a bit, but at that point, I was already an orange belt in karate. Still, I knew I would pay for this fight twice. The second time would occur later in the week when I had to tell Bill, my karate teacher, that I'd been in another fight.

Here they were, right on schedule. There were five today – four boys and their leader, a girl named Nicole. Funny enough,

Nicole was Afro-German, too – she just had much less "Afro" in her than in me so that she could hide the similarity. Then there was Volker and three other guys I did not know. I had to hit Volker with everything I had and get the others to think twice before they came for a piece of me. That was my usual strategy: identify the strongest, and make him hurt as much as possible. If the most formidable attacker felt some pain and hopefully cried, I had won. There were moral, psychological, and physical victories. In second grade, I often started to win all categories. There were not too many seven-year-olds with multiple years of rigorous Shotokan Karate education under their belts. The better I got at hurting my attackers, the older the assailants became, and there were more of them. I eventually lost my fear of older kids. I was fearless, arrogant, and angry, with a short fuse.

They had a plan. It wasn't Volker this time; the weaker ones tried to attack me first. I guess Volker was still hurting from the day before yesterday. Good – I had a plan too. I set to helping those three losers understand that it was a mistake to even think about hitting this Neger.

I am Black, and I am proud, just like my mum taught me. And I can fight like the only Black Karate teacher in town taught me. When I replay those days in my head now, it reminds me of a blaxploitation movie. The language was different, but the plot was the same. This Black kid exploited a few eight-year-olds back to their mummies that day. But it was just another day in the neighborhood for (almost) the only Black kid in town.

AM I MY BROTHER'S KEEPER?

Race came up again when I joined the German Army because I was one of the few Black guys there. Unfortunately, another person in my unit fed the negative stereotypes. His conduct annoyed me because I felt weirdly responsible for his behavior.

This odd feeling of responsibility for someone else's actions is a notion only minorities can understand. We were both Afro-German; why should I feel responsible for another dude who happened to share a single superficial identifier with me? Black. A Neger – a word in Germany that had already made the list of non-politically correct terms by the mid-1990s. I was twenty years old at the time and a soldier in the German Army's psychological operations

> Brother's Keeper is a movement started by Afro-German musicians and artists in the late 1990s to create awareness of Germany's racial divide. Brother's Keeper is such a strong concept that Barack Obama used it to launch his Brothers' Keeper foundation twenty years later.
>
> Coincidence? Well, it is unclear whether the German movement inspired Obama's choice, but it is possible. Obama's sister lives in Berlin, where many of the German movement's active members also live.

unit. I was a PsyOp and still felt responsible for another person's behavior.

Final day in Sarajevo, Bosnia; 1st Contingent SFOR, May 1997

I did not realize the importance of my
PsyOp experience to my life's overall story until
much later. Understanding and analyzing

*my opponent turned out to be a useful notion.
Let's put a pin in that discussion for now.*

The responsibility I felt back then still creeps into my life today, even though I know it is ridiculous. I am well-educated, and I understand why people end up where they are. That burden of responsibility hits me – even in New York City, once the epicenter of the dream of freedom, equality, and Black power. New York City was indeed that for the teenage me back in Germany, who watched Black movies like *New Jack City* and listened to music from Ice T, Eric B. & Rakim, and Public Enemy. That feeling of responsibility strikes me now in 2021, over a good ten years after moving to the New York Metro area (a fancy name for the New Jersey side of the Hudson River). You may wonder if I moved to NYC in the hope of becoming free and explore my Black side finally. But no, when I moved to New York, I was aware of who and what I am. I had quite literally fought the battles and had the scars to prove it. I felt good.

But was I? When I first arrived in New York, I got that responsible feeling whenever I saw a person of color acting in a way that could be labeled as "misbehaving" (there is much to explore in that sentence, but let's leave it for now).

It took me many years and lessons to finally let that feeling go. The more I learned about what it truly meant to be Black in the United States of America, the more I understood how people got to where they were. Everyone struggled, just in vastly distinct ways. If you are Black, Brown, yellow, or red (who fabricated these color designations anyway?), society dealt you a bad hand. It was just a question of how bad and whether it would continue. It turns out that suppression is an equal-opportunity offender, and gender, religion, race, sexuality, or any other perceived difference are not immune. Everyone is welcome at that club.

I started looking at things from different perspectives during my time in New York (Metro, I know). I began to feel the same anger and attitude I'd had in my childhood. My time in the United States reminded me of the many events that brought me there and made me the person asking this question: What must change to make racism stop? I also asked myself why I was back in a situation where everything is about race after I thought I was done with it. Is it time for us to take responsibility? For us Black people to become the engines that force change and finally get ourselves out of this mess?

Over the decades, I remodeled myself from a kid who lived solely to defeat the leader of an enemy force to a person who is now well-educated and well-paid. I have an exciting career, a brilliant wife, and a cute son. I now only worry about proving things to myself. Finally, I determine my self-worth. I am still a driven and competitive person, and I love learning. I strive and wonder what else I can achieve. A new master's degree? Or two? Can I write a book? Or two or three? I am finally having fun simply because I compete against myself.

My great life would be even better if it weren't for the real world. And so, the frustration rises, and I think, "If only I could breathe."

Why do police officers shoot Black people left and right and get away with it?

Why do so many Black people make themselves a target? Why are we targets in the first place? Why can't we breathe? Why aren't we allowed to breathe?

How will this nightmare end?

What must we do to own the change because no one else cares enough to change this harmful situation?

How did I remove myself from this equation and become "not a target?" Is this even true, or have I made it far enough that this is just an illusion? Do I have to get involved? Do I have to become my brothers' and sisters' keeper?

I wrote this book to explore racism and help us all find answers and solutions. I honestly thought I was done with this. Now that my son is five, I feel driven to make racism and suppression stop. I need to figure out how we can work together to eliminate discrimination or create a significant turnaround.

For our children's sake, racial suppression must stop. We must act.

If we want to get our breath back, we must take it back.

FIGHTING BACK

I was born in Trier, a small city with a lot of potential in southwestern Germany, near the Luxembourg border. The former center of the Roman Empire's northernmost part, Trier has many well-preserved Roman structures telling a tale of past greatness. In the mid-seventies, however, those buildings were the only thing great about it.

Because it is close to the Luxembourg border and a garrison city, French soldiers had their barracks in town. On weekends, however, the many American soldiers stationed in the villages and small towns in the surrounding area dominated the city, coming to marvel at two thousand years of history they could touch. Some of those military bases are still active today.

In the 1970s, American soldiers and their families made up more than seventy percent of Spangdahlem, Bitburg, and Bad Homburg. And the locals hated it. Racism was high, and I was in the middle of the tensions. The son of an American soldier and a German local, I felt the heat, and so did my mother. My birth father was never in the picture; instead, a (White) German man stepped in who could not relate to the topic of racism. How could he? That meant my mum and I dealt with it on our own.

Together, we met sideways looks, open stares, head shakes, hurtful comments, and churches that would not baptize me.

That may not sound like much, but the churches ran the daycares, and if church officials wouldn't baptize you, you could not attend daycare. Fortunately, my mum's boss and one of her two mentors came to our aid. An influential monk of the "Barmherzigen Brüder" order made sure I was baptized and ordered a daycare to take me in when I was very young.

The daily fights at daycare started as soon as I became old enough to be a "person." It was so bad that my mum showed me how to make a fist. She instilled a "Black is powerful" mentality in me and taught me how to fight back and not take anything from anyone. I was naturally strong, and I got quite a workout from fighting every day. As the fights grew more intense, so did my anger.

But my daily brawls were just part of the problem. In some parts of the city, people threw stones at our car as we drove by, and they saw me, a Black boy. In this city of barely a hundred thousand people, half the town was entirely off-limits, the other half ranging from passive-aggressive to openly hostile. Because of my history, I can relate to the United States' tragic videos in the 1960s. I experienced it every single day between the ages of three to eight.

When my mum's friend suggested I join his dojo and learn karate, things started to turn around. My teacher, William "Bill" Marsh, was an instructor in Trier. An Afro-American from the U.S. South, a well-known lead singer for a local band, a third-degree black belt, and married to a local woman with two kids, Bill knew what I was going through. He also knew I needed his brand of education: how to be Black in White surroundings.

Legend had it that the KKK burned down Bill's parental home. He had seen it all, yet he had an astonishing relaxed and robust aura about him. My mum decided I needed to learn to maneuver my environment as Bill did. Nobody in town messed with him – a reputation about town for being a third-degree black belt will do that for you. If you messed with Bill, you were ridiculed or wore the marks that told the story and sent a message: do not mess with Bill Marsh. When I was six or seven years old, I started Bill's karate classes.

MY RESPONSIBILITY OR MY FIGHTS, MY FAULT

Bill's children, a boy and a girl, were four and one years older than me, respectively. Of course, growing up with a professional, they were advanced karate practitioners and talented. For the sake of my karate lessons, Bill adopted me. I received the same scrutiny he gave his children. We were the only Black kids in his classes, and we had to be the best and most disciplined at everything. Bill made sure we were not sloppy or out of shape and that we did not rush form. If we didn't correctly bow when we entered the dojo, that earned us ten push-ups. Jump on the training mat without a proper bow – ten push-ups. Sloppy with any exercises or wrong more than twice – ten push-ups. If we tried to cheat on the push-ups, we'd get ten more, plus the initial ten. Bill's push-ups were the good hard ones, too – on the knuckles. They became our currency. Coincidently, I got good at them.

Bill's push-up regime also taught me discipline. The first karate test allowing me to move to the next belt taught me how demanding Bill was. To earn my first belt, I had to execute a series of choreographed moves. The form, tempo, expression, and intensity had to be one hundred percent on point. Somehow, I failed, which meant I got less than ninety-eight. Bill only allowed me to get the white-yellow belt, saying I was not ready for the full yellow because of my daily fights.

Bill said I was not mentally ready for my first belt because my exercises were sloppy and aggressive. From then on, I had to report my fights to Bill. I still fought every day; now, however, I was in elementary school and faced more assailants who were older. I also had more opportunities to fight – both on the way to and at kindergarten itself – and became even stronger from all the karate, push-ups, and aggression. The number of my opponents increased because I was strong, and it took more than just two or three to handle my moves.

Bill wanted to hear about my altercations, including every detail. He always had one question: what did I do to prevent them?

What, me? Did you not listen? They attacked me. You should be proud! I got two or three of them good. They will not attack me again. I flashed a proud smile. Well, at least the first time I told the story. Then I learned not to be proud of my fights or keep score.

Bill said, "You had the fights. You are not here in karate classes to learn how to fight. The strength we teach here is not how to physically beat up and defeat your opponents. You must dissolve the fights before they happen. You win fights mentally."

I was confused and asked, "Uhm, how can I do this when they just start attacking me?"

"Defend, but do not be the aggressor. Show your attackers why they should stop. Dissolve and de-escalate the situation. You must learn to control your anger and the situation. Now, burn off all that energy with thirty push-ups," Bill instructed.

I was not able to do much about the fights. I tried to tell my attackers it would end badly for at least two or three of them, but talking did not help. First, they would laugh, and then they would just increase the number of kids who confronted me. As the number of push-ups I was assigned increased, so did my aggression. I wanted to hurt those racist kids as much as I humanly could.

In the spring before my eighth birthday, I wore an orange belt (I had to go through yellow, yellow/orange, to orange – he made these up, didn't he?), and I had a defining moment. A set of kids always had to clean the yard at school, and this would rotate. On this day, when I was in second grade, it was me, a classmate of mine, and two fourth graders. They started by first looking at me, then saying things, and then pushing me. I lost it badly. Teachers came and tried to hold me back. It took several to constrain me, and they also got a share of my aggression. The two fourth graders had unplanned visits to the dentist; the tooth fairy did not come to collect their front teeth.

This incident got an incredible amount of attention throughout the school, with its officials calling my mum in for a chat and attacking her: what kind of son did she have? They claimed they had never seen this level of brutality. If not for Brother Benedict, officials would have kicked me out of school. Instead, kids kept their distance. I had won. For now, all the kids were afraid of me.

You might think, "Good!"

No. Bad. Karate teacher Bill was not happy. I lost my orange belt and went back to yellow, the scrutiny to perfect everything increasing.

BIGGER CITY, BIGGER MINDS

Things were not working out in Trier, so my mum decided we had to move to Cologne, a much bigger and far more diverse city. It was also where my stepfather had family members I liked, including kids from his first marriage. Shortly after we moved, the youngest of the two, Markus, became my best friend.

I also went to a new school. I was determined to make sure I would no longer go through any of this. I would beat up anyone who looked at me funny – badly, too. I would not become anyone's punching bag again. Yet, there was something new about this; something odd about these kids made them different than those from my early childhood. It took me several weeks, if not months, to fully understand what that was.

They did not care about my skin color and just took me as I was – well, once I stopped beating them up. These kids, like me, were not necessarily all German. Their parents were Italian, Turkish, African, and so on. Everyone was from somewhere; I was just one of them. I had never experienced anything like it. What was with all these other nationalities? All I had known were Germans, U.S. Americans, and French. There was more, huh? Interesting.

CLEAN THE MIND

Cologne changed everything. If people looked at me, it was because they were curious, interested, and friendly. Nobody cared much about my skin color other than that they were jealous that I did not need to get a tan. They liked my hair and Jackson 5-style afro.

I learned much about people and positive prejudice in those years. My look suddenly became an advantage if I wanted it to be. People always remembered me and my name. And people liked me. This life was all very new.

I learned what made them tick and what made them feel comfortable. For the first time in my life, I wanted to be part of the group instead of fighting or daring them to be brave enough to attack me. Nobody wanted to do so anymore, and not because they were scared – I might have been a fierce nine-year-old, but I was still just that. Still doing karate, I was finally old enough and in a less volatile situation that Bill Marsh's prevention tactics started working. I was much stronger than anyone else at my age, too – all those push-ups.

Something else was different with the new karate dojo. Here, again, I was just one of the kids. Sure, I was much younger than anyone else at my level. I started to advance through the belts, too, since I no longer have to do the half-steps with what seemed made-up color combinations. I left karate with a brown belt at age twelve; it just wasn't the same anymore. The people around me were old – over twenty. Also, I no longer needed it. I'd had my last fight (if that's even the right word) at age ten: a single half-power slap that the boy took like I was Mike Tyson. That altercation ended my fighting days. It even felt weird to hit someone now, and I have never punched, slapped, or kicked anyone since. Some of it was luck; I was around the right people or just fortunate circumstances. Most of the changes came from Bill Marsh's lessons. I used his grip techniques and holds so effectively that it changed my opponents' minds about their next steps.

Instead of fighting, I quickly became a guy people liked. Everywhere. Always. I learned the local dialect and mastered it well enough to amaze others. I started to be a typical teenager and as happy as one is at that age. Compared to what I'd gone through, most things were a piece of cake now. Every day I was on the go with my best friend, Markus. Race stopped being a topic for me, and this calmed me down just in time to attend the next level of school. For fifth grade, I would go to "Liebfrauenschule," and that changed things significantly.

EDUCATION AND PERSPECTIVE

Liebfrauenschule was led by nuns and one of the strictest and toughest schools around. It was also private, which meant that they had more funds available and accepted donations, but thankfully no tuition costs were involved; we would not have been able to afford it anyway. Still, the kids who attended came from upper-middle-class or were merely rich, with family drivers dropping a few off at school. Bullying over no money was not an issue because everyone had it (minus my parents and me), so where was the fun?

We all struggled to adhere to the school's exacting demands it set for students. Everyone expected us to do well, attend university, and get high-paying jobs – just like their parents. No one here looked at blue-collar jobs as a possibility. These were future scholars, bankers, doctors, or entrepreneurs. Nothing less. For those who were not ready for the challenge and pace, there was an extra session called "silentium" (Latin for "imposed" silence) – a daily, two-hour after-school class to focus on homework or studying for upcoming tests.

Liebfrauenschule was the first time I met this type of person, and I struggled mightily. Not because I felt lesser or uncomfortable with fellow students but because I struggled to adjust to the pace, challenge, and singular focus those kids had. Most took it in stride, their parents pushing them to ensure their success. My mum raised me on her own while working a demanding job, so she had neither had the time nor energy to stay on top of things like the other parents did – they were stay-at-home mums or had nannies, au pairs, and support systems unimaginable for us, let alone reachable.

Although I struggled through my five years at that school, my time there taught me to expect more of myself. Of course I would study. Of course I would succeed. Of course, of course, of course. All I had to do was find my way.

Then, when I was fifteen, my mum was in an accident. She was in and out of the hospital for more than a year. Although my stepfather was technically around, I lived alone and managed the household. During this period, I got off track and left school after not getting my certification to attend university. I had lost the guidance and environment keeping me focused on my education.

Today, I appreciate how crucial that time was and how vital direction is for any child, especially during the turbulent teenage years. I now understand how my time at Liebfrauenschule helped me gain the perspective many of my new friends lacked. Still, this detour took me off-course for several years and opened me up to the well-known scrutiny from the outside. These were the early 1990s, shortly after the Berlin Wall had fallen. With the East opening, racism suddenly became a topic again. But this time, I was no longer a six-year-old. I was much older and ready.

RUMBLE AND TUMBLE OF BLACK TEENAGERS IN GERMANY

We are all in search of identity in our mid-teenage years. We all try to figure out who we are and who we want to be. We still don't have control over our bodies and try to figure out what to do with it.

For a Black kid in Germany, these identity crises went a little further. Racism's resurgence in Germany reminded me that I was not like everyone else around me. If the years at Liebfrauenschule had almost allowed me to forget how I was different, I became painstakingly aware of it again. But now, I found people who looked like me – what a diverse bunch of people it was. My group (we weren't a gang at all) were a mix of people from many different African countries, a few Americans, South Americans, and Germans. The Germans usually had one local parent and the other from somewhere else in the world. We would hang out, play ball, go to parties, or spend time together. Education was not a topic. Neither was the future. These years were all about the moment – the then and now.

Some of the kids who had dreadful backgrounds and no perspective drove this attitude. They eventually graduated to criminal acts that cost them their freedom or more. I am still surprised that I never joined anything like this; instead, I attribute the values instilled in me by my mum and the environment she created for me, like my previous school. Her guidance saved me from losing my way and gave me an inner compass that kept me on a positive path. Our group began to split.

Some took a grave turn for the worse, while others created and used their energy for something positive. We became musicians, dancers, and creatives, spending our time learning and challenging each other to better our craft. When I look back, we all built on that experience and made at least a solid hobby, if not a living out of that positive energy. We pulled ourselves out of the negativity and looked for perspective. In a slightly changed setting, this group defined much of Germany's music and television landscape in the mid to late-1990s. We became music artists, TV VJs at MTV, or the German pendant VIVA. We became DJs and music producers or shifted to the music industry's business side, like me. However, before I got there, I took a couple more detours that eventually set me on my correct course.

I did not get my university certificate because I started a UPS job a few days after my eighteenth birthday. My stepfather had challenged me to follow his will, or he would withdraw financial support. "Fine, I'll get my own money," was my response to his demands that were straight from 1950's Germany. I had a job that paid me around a thousand Marks – about five hundred US dollars. That was in 1993 and a lot of money for an eighteen-year-old, but it also meant I worked every day from five pm to eight pm or later, depending on the season.

These hours also meant I was often tired.

I was too tired to get up in the morning for school and too tired to do much homework; I didn't have the time. This experience taught me one thing, and it was a profound lesson: physical work is hard. At age nineteen, I had just completed the twelfth grade and failed it for the second time. I left school and worked full-time for a year. That year was the most challenging time of my life as I switched to the early shift to make more money. Now I worked from quarter to five in the morning until two or three pm. If I wanted to meet friends or hang out with them, it meant I went a night without sleep. That also meant I would go straight to bed after work the next day.

I learned a life lesson during this time. I decided it could not continue, but I had no idea how to disrupt the cycle. I was tired most of the time and could not even think about getting my certification. My perspective narrowed. Fortunately, my friendships gave me a vision beyond my work. I saw what my friends were doing and started to join them when I could. I wanted to become more than I was at the time. Enter ambition.

I learned many lessons during the years at UPS. For one, I learned to work with my hands. It was arduous work that exhausted me as much as the long work hours did. Delivering packages, I also met people from all levels of society. They had their own stories, situations, preferences, fears, likes, and dislikes. My earlier experiences instinctively allowed me to relate to people and adjust. I knew how to behave around different people and do things they could relate to and appreciate. I was neat, polite, and respected them – no questions asked. Although this seems like a one-way deal, it also meant those people would do the same for me. They would use their forklifts to load my UPS truck for me if they had multiple pallets, or coffee or sandwiches would be waiting for me. Customers that other drivers found disrespectful, unfriendly, or even racist became the very customers I liked to go to the most because they were not like that with me.

One driver once took me on his route during Christmas – an intense season for any parcel service, even before online shopping services like Amazon and eBay. Arriving at one customer, he held me back and wanted to deliver the package himself. "This customer has a reputation for being very rude to people who do not fit his ideals," he said. I told the driver I would be all right, and he could come in with me.

When I walked in, I heard the customer speak in the local dialect, complaining about people who no longer had proper manners. So, as politely as I could, I addressed him in his dialect. With a broad smile, I looked him straight in his eyes. The man's face changed about forty times in two seconds until finally, an even wider smile appeared. "My good boy, come here and put this package right there. This is how things are done, you see?" Directed at my colleague, "This young fellow knows how to treat people with respect. What a nice young guy." To me, "Do you want a coffee or anything? It is cold outside, and you guys must be frozen solid by now."

For the rest of that day and many after, my colleague looked at me like I knew witchcraft. He had never seen this guy be anything even remotely resembling friendly, let alone downright forthcoming and happy. My coworker had seen this customer kick out and cuss at other people before, but I turned him around to be like the nice grandfather next door.

I told my colleague, "You have to understand the guy, respect his environment, and make him feel comfortable. That is all. It's simply basic human needs."

"The hell it is. Witchcraft is what you used," he said with a loud laugh. He told that story to anyone who would listen.

Then, another detour once again disrupted my entire life: the German Army drafted me to a unit called Opi – whatever that was.

German Army

I never thought I would join the German Army – it was always a given that I would take the alternative route and do a social services year somewhere. Still, constant exhaustion can cause you to miss a few deadlines and removes a lot of initiative. And so, on July 3rd, 1996, I drove to Mayen, Germany. It was only about sixty miles from home, but it might as well have been on the other side of the world. There was nothing. Naturally, the base was not close to Mayen's small city but another few miles away in what turned out to be bad-weather central. If you've ever heard of the Nürburgring, you also know of the challenging weather situation there. My base was just a few hills away and a few meters higher. While I learned to deal with snow in May, it was by far not the most crucial lesson awaiting me during the next three years and two months (yes, I served a little longer than the mandatory ten months). I was now a soldier.

This OPI unit turned out to be OpInfo, short for "Operational Information," like the U.S. Psychological Operations (PsyOps).

OpInfo focused on creating immediate and short-term behavioral changes in opponents by utilizing what would now be called a "data-driven multi-media" campaign. We used flyers, magazines, radio, or announcements via capable speakers to motivate our opponents to do what we wanted.

To be able to do this, we studied a great deal on human behavior and motivation. We learned about empathy and how to use the power of listening, watching, and collecting data to understand our target audience better. I was now learning the theoretical basics of what I had been instinctively doing for years. My time at OpInfo trained me to change my perspective on life, allowing me to focus on my opposition rather than on myself. Suddenly, my behavior was no longer the only factor determining and driving any situation's outcome. I had learned that I needed to know as much as possible in as little time as possible about my opposition to anticipate their behavior and how they might react to me and my actions. These strategies and tactics paved the way for my marketing career and becoming a leader, shaping how I deal with people every day. I learned how to diffuse any situation in the best way, if I wanted to. I also learned to create a calculated escalation whenever that worked for my benefit.

Learning the tools that make OpInfo and PsyOps successful worldwide helped me become successful in my daily life. A young man of twenty-one must learn plenty of lessons that have nothing to do with Psychological Operations theories. But this education gave me an essential shift in my reality.

Not everything was about me. Not all offensive behavior is because of how I look, my skin color, or any single factor. Even racial slurs often have nothing to do with me. Insults are frequently rooted in people's fears or weaknesses or as a result of jealousy or enormous external pressure. I started to preempt and counteract potential behavior with how I spoke, meaning I used dialect, talked more loudly or more softly, and looked people straight in the eye. I also smiled at people. It didn't matter who or what they were – I surprised them, and they remembered me for my skills and who I was as a person, not how I looked. Okay, if the person was a smart and pretty girl and remembered how I looked, that also wasn't a bad thing – after all, I was twenty-one and confident on a different level.

Much like with UPS, again, the German Army introduced me to many different people I would never have met otherwise. It also introduced me to situations more than foreign to me. While there, I did two tours in Bosnia as part of the multi-national NATO forces. My OpInfo group teamed up with the U.S. PsyOps and similar teams from other nations, like Italy, France, Russia, and the U.K. We mainly worked in a German-American team due to our responsibilities. I learned more about Americans and discovered that I liked them – they were fun and a remarkably diverse bunch of likable girls and guys. Because I got along well with Americans – and being the only one who understood what they were saying – I teamed up with my captain and became the link to the American and international teams. While with them, I was just one of the soldiers until we went out to meet people. It was there I learned more about being authentic than at any other time in life.

When meeting local people to gather information, they frequently looked at me in the German uniform and stopped cold in their tracks. They did not believe I was German; they thought I was a spy.

Germans were well-liked in Bosnia by all three ethnic groups – unlike American or French soldiers, whom locals perceived as imperialistic occupants. To them, I was an American spy pretending to be German to get information. The locals did not warm to my aspiration to be as American as I could. They saw me as a fraud. It was an amusing twist to my non-German-looking narrative. Suddenly, I had to prove I was German for entirely new reasons, and I started to carry my German passport around in addition to my ID card. It became part of my routine to show my German passport in these situations.

In camp, our OpInfo group was also unique. We were the shiny and popular group with the local soldier radio and supplied critical intelligence to the leadership. As such, any prominent visitor came by our barracks – generals, politicians, they all visited, or we had to show up to their gatherings. As the only Black guy in the group and one of a handful of several thousand German soldiers in the camp, I always had to attend sessions focused on racism in the German Army. It was not a big topic for me since my unit was vastly different from the fighting companies whose members were recruited more for their physical abilities than school smarts.

The only racist incident that occurred came at the most opportune time. I used this incident to exit the Army to pursue another career and help my friends build and grow Panthertainment – a marketing and model agency and TV production company.

BLACK-OWNED AGENCY

Core team of early Panthertainment days; (l-r):
Maurice, Lucienne, Marco, Tyron, Dee

Driven and creative, a few of us Afro-German guys founded and built Panthertainment. We initially centered the business around a hip-hop TV show that one of us, Tyron Ricketts, hosted. It quickly became a trendsetting agency designed to counteract the experience Tyron and others had as models or actors in a growing urban media landscape. Although Germany was becoming more diverse in the 1990s, most of society still clung to narrow stereotypes. Studios cast Black people as either athletes, musicians, or criminals – or a combination of the three, if possible. There also wasn't room for more than one Black role. "This isn't Harlem," was the attitude, and not much has changed since then.

However, we did not accept these restrictions and fought them. Interestingly, both industry executives and Black talent often shared these racial biases, feeling more comfortable in their traditional roles.

Just as White Germany wasn't ready to let us in, our fellow Black Germans weren't ready to let us go. There was a clear generational divide. Only a few years older than us, these Black Germans could not have been more different. From their perspective, being Black was about surviving and dealing with victimhood. On the other hand, we expected people to deal with us. Since we worked in media and were highly visible, we were trendsetters for the youth and young adults – Black, White, and every shade in between. People knew us, and we liked it – a lot. We were in our early twenties and enjoyed being young, Black, and famous (in our niche). We wanted to challenge the status quo, and it did not matter who was setting it.

GERMAN HIP-HOP HISTORY – HOW I MET U.S. RAP LEGENDS

We based our idea of what Black people (at least the cool ones) were supposed to be on images and impressions that extended hip-hop culture gave us. We were influenced by movies like *Do the Right Thing; Boyz n the Hood; Menace to Society*, and *New Jack City*, as well as the MTV show *Yo MTV Raps,* and hip-hop music in general. We learned what it meant to be Black and struggling in a White society. Suddenly, our role models looked like us, and we learned to talk like them – well, kind of. We had to pick up a lot more English, and we had to shake the German accent or British English we learned in school. We all picked up the hip-hop culture one way or another, from rapping, DJing, break dancing, graffiti, or fashion. We were no longer just consumers of hip-hop culture – we had created our local version, becoming pioneers and close followers of a hip-hop movement that slowly but surely took over Germany and Europe.

When Tyron (one of Panthertainment's founders) hosted a show called *Word Cup* on a German music TV channel, VIVA TV, other Panthertainment members became involved. I handled the second camera or translated international guest interviews into

German. I was still with the German Army but spent weekends at the TV station learning how to edit on machines that one can now only find in a museum. I learned how to do TV from the ground up in my free time, either after hours or on weekends. I asked the professional editors to show me how things operated and helped them by doing assistants' work, like returning tapes to the archive. I wanted to learn all aspects of the process.

Word Cup ran from the 1990s until 2007. Eventually, Panthertainment produced the entire show. When Jens Scope Kameke, the man who had the only hip-hop TV show older than ours, joined our team, it seemed like we were unstoppable. All the top hip-hop artists appeared on our show: Jay-Z, LL Cool J, Lauryn Hill, Ice T, De La Soul, Guru – all of them. We also created a platform for German hip-hop artists who suddenly became visible because of us. During this time, in 1998 and 1999, we made a popular and commercially successful version of German hip-hop culture. What Tyron wore on Sunday kids dragged their parents to streetwear stores to buy on Monday.

My work on Word Cup brought me to New York for the first time in February 1999. We had interviews scheduled around the anniversary of Tommy Boy Records and with NAS. The week was a whirlwind of impressions for me that started in Mase of De La Soul's home on Long Island, where we planned to do the first interview. While I waited for the interview to start, we played PlayStation and NBA Live – me as this skinny kid from Germany repeatedly beating one of Mase's buddies. From there, it just got crazier and crazier.

When we drove to Manhattan for the first time, a series of interviews and sessions there and in Brooklyn kept me on my heels and my head on a swivel. I loved it. I also experienced one of the funniest moments in my young adult life on that trip. While we waited for Tyron's friend at Bad Boy Records, we were invited to a little party in the West Village that night. We all decided to go. *This is like a video*, I thought when we got to the club. It was small but super cool. Everyone was either extremely good-looking or had major swagger – most had both. We sat at a table, noticing the beautiful girls who sat across from us on a couch. After a few minutes, it started to feel a little weird. Tyron's friend did not show up, and no one noticed us. The girls on the couch did not even look at or around us but just stared through us; we felt invisible.

A woman finally informed us that our friend had canceled, but she would take care of us. She asked where we were from and why we were in New York, so we told her we produced a German TV hip-hop show and worked with De La Soul and NAS, to name a few. She reacted as though we had merely recited a grocery list.

Then, when Puffy walked in, it made sense, and our confidence built back up a little. In short, this was not an ordinary

Meeting Spike Lee in Berlin, Germany. Late 1990's

evening at the club, even for New York, as we learned that we were at an exclusive industry party. Pheeeewww!

This anecdote is my favorite to tell, showing how one can feel so important and then so deflated within minutes or seconds because of your surroundings.

Eventually, the TV station wanted to regain control and canceled the show in late 1999. We lacked the skills to keep the network executives happy and moved our operation to a local radio station for a few months, eventually stopping in late 2004.

By then, the company had changed, and so had the environment. The internet was fast becoming a crucial source of multimedia entertainment. I had assumed the role of CEO about a year earlier, and during a midnight work session, I wrote the rough outline for an idea that eventually brought *Word Cup* back to the screen. It aired first on the internet, then on TV.

Selcuk Erdogan hosted the German interviews, and I did the international ones, streaming the show on hiphop.de. We were first again, and again we changed the German hip-hop scene. Tyron's cameos initially helped, but this was a different show now. We became a platform for German hip-hop culture, and it gave us freedom. We interviewed who we wanted and decided how to do it. We ran video interviews with German, European, and American hip-hop stars. They all came back. I interviewed whoever made the trip over the pond during those years – LL Cool J, 50 Cent, Method Man, De La Soul, Shaggy, Guru, Ciara – all the top stars at that time.

Meeting…(l-r, t-b) DJ Premier, Guru & Solar, Chamillionaire,
Dj Jazzy Jeff, , 50 Cent, Ciara, LL Cool J (below)

A few of the interview guests of the re-started Word Cup show, 2005-2007.

I understood and related to my childhood idols. I learned their image in front of the camera and on stage was different from their private life. Just like us, they had grown up. They were brands that had to be managed and sustained. I always wondered if the kids who listened to the music knew how much work went into the craft of hip-hop entertainment. It took real professionalism to maintain successful careers, some of which started in the 1980s and still thrive in the 2000s.

In our interviews, the artists revealed how they had to learn, get degrees, and become insiders in a White-owned industry – one that is still dominated by White people today. They became professionals and took charge of their destinies to develop into the international icons many are today.

These were valuable lessons for me, but Panthertainment was in trouble. Although we'd had remarkable success, we were not the best business strategists and accountants in the world. We had an impressive list of customers like Siemens, Ubisoft, Nike, Dodge, Sony Playstation, Reebok, and German-based record companies, plus most of their movie publishing peers. However, we were too green behind the ears and lacked the acumen to understand proper pricing and run a sustainable business. We struggled to keep our company afloat and only barely did so in the final years, but we did change some essential aspects of the German media landscape. We positioned Black people outside of clichés, introduced and pioneered online-based music television, and introduced the American brand of street promotion to Germany.

I realized schooling was a crucial piece to any success. Although I could land executive jobs at small software companies, I knew I had to further my education. I ended up earning an MBA from Liverpool University's online program while working full time.

The Hard Way – MBA

Studying for my MBA at Liverpool University was the best thirty thousand euros I'd ever spent. It was also the most challenging thirteen months of my professional career but well worth it. I learned a lot about the business world but even more about myself. I could do anything I wanted, and nothing could stop me if I made up my mind and pushed through. Of course, I needed to ask for help along the way. My wife, Saskia, helped me through one especially nasty math assignment due in 24 hours. Math was never my strongest subject, and there was a chance I didn't listen or attend the necessary lessons during my earlier school years. It was clear I missed the groundwork for this delightful assignment when working for UPS. After a few angry, panicky hours, I eventually locked myself in my home office and chugged away at the problem. I finally went to bed at six the following morning and could rest because I knew I had fought this assignment and brought it to its knees. After a few hours of sleep, I submitted it one hour before the deadline – a real victory for me.

Getting an advanced degree like an MBA achieved something else for me – I became part of the club. Before I obtained my degree, when anyone asked me for education credentials, I had to ramble about my agency background, TV productions, and other on-the-job experiences. I could not claim that I had higher education experience. The MBA from a British University changed that for me. It opened doors to new jobs and new perspectives, even though I never had to show my actual certificate to anyone. With the MBA, I learned about the power of education. I uncovered insider terms and phrases. I can talk-the-talk and use proper tools.

Most notably, in a stunning change, I caught the education bug and will to keep learning. I still have that drive – whether I'm researching and reading on my own, attaching myself to good role models, or taking online courses. I am always learning something new. Today, I am about to finish another certificate course and have applied for a dual-masters program at Syracuse University.

WELCOME TO THE U.S.A.

In 2010, my pharmaceutical-executive fiancée at the time (now-wife) had the opportunity to work in the U.S. for three years as an expatriate. I was working at a startup I had founded, focused on marketing patents for alternative energy technologies. At the time, multiple companies in that sector faced significant financing problems. We were no different, so I didn't hesitate to follow my wife and move to my favorite city in the United States – New York.

After an eye-opening experience during our week of house hunting, moving to New York meant living in New Jersey, just north of Manhattan and across the George Washington Bridge.

By proxy of my wife, I had finally made it. I was living in New York (metropolitan area). We had barely arrived when we started to explore the city. Manhattan, Brooklyn, Queens, the Bronx – these urban centers offered us new experiences. Our hometown was one of the biggest in Germany, with a population of one million, but that was less than any one of New York City's five boroughs. Everything about this city made an impression on us. We noticed how big Manhattan was and how different compared to the other boroughs. We noted the people on the streets and quickly learned we weren't particularly special – nobody was, for that matter. Did you think you were the tallest, smallest, biggest, skinniest, blackest, whitest, richest, poorest, or most or least exciting person on Earth? Well, just around the next corner, you could meet someone who was that times ten. That was liberating for me. Suddenly, I wasn't the Black guy anymore. Suddenly, hundreds looked just like me on the very street I walked. I could hide in plain sight, relax, and feel a freedom I had never felt before. I felt at home, four thousand miles from where I had spent most of my life. There was hip-hop music on the radio, entire stations playing hip-hop, soul, or gospel music. I no longer had to research and go out of my way to find like-minded people. I confirmed my exciting experiences during my first trip to New York in 1999, and then some.

About a year after we moved to the U.S., I started working for a German software company based in Olpe, Germany. I eventually became a member of the company's U.S. team, tasked with local marketing for the U.S. salesforce and, more importantly, starting their customer success program. With that, I traveled around the U.S. often. I saw a new city and state every month for three years. I started to learn about the U.S. and the country's positive and negative aspects. I began to understand the differences between the various regions and their mentalities. I visited places like Provo, UT; Kansas City, MO; Louisville, KY; Sunnyvale, CA; Boulder, CO; Nashville, TN; Miami, FL; Jackson, MS; Jackson, AL; San Antonio, TX; Minneapolis, MN; Burlington, MA; Indianapolis, IN; Greenville, SC; and Roanoke, VA. I got around and saw the real United States beyond New York and Los Angeles.

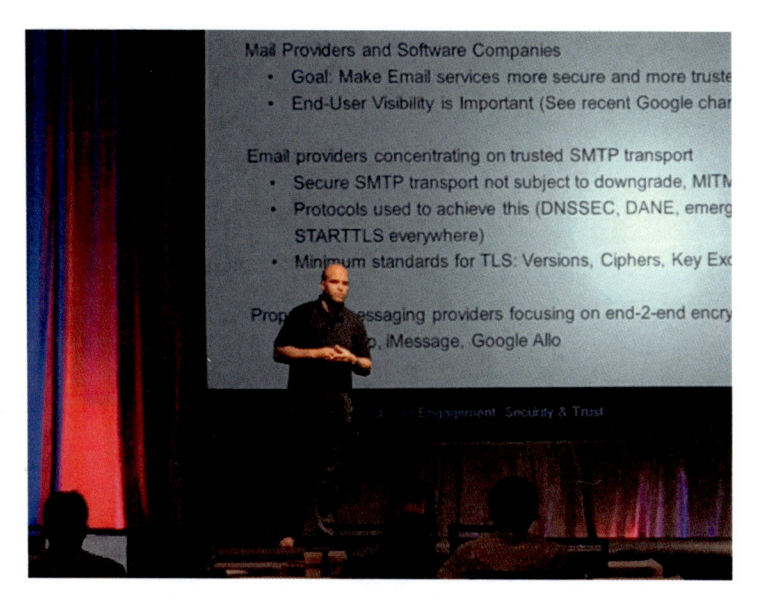

Speaking at a tech event in Phoenix, AZ; 2016

I came to appreciate the various regions' differences and commonalities. I finally understood why the U.S. and many Americans seem self-centered, never leaving the United States: the country is enormous. You can get on a plane in the U.S., fly six hours, and still be in the same country on touchdown. In Germany, we barely fly an hour and land in another nation. There is probably only one in-country German airplane route that takes ninety minutes. A six-hour flight takes you well out of Europe; you can get from Moscow to Lisbon – one end of the continent to the other – in about five and a half hours, only hanging in the air for three or four if you limit your travels to the European Union. That flight gets you into another country with a different language and sometimes even another currency.

The U.S.'s geographic size is something to behold to a European, let alone a German guy from Cologne, where Luxemburg, Holland, Belgium, and France are less than a two-hour drive away.

I quickly learned there are differences in the various regions. People told us to be careful if going to Brooklyn or Harlem and the South and Midwest because it may not be safe for a mixed couple. These concerns sounded like Trier in the 1970s. Luckily, we didn't have any bad experiences.

Racism – I thought I was done with this

It is not that Germany is a racism-free zone – not by a long shot. Everyday racism happens in Germany just as much as it does in the U.S – it's just that it occurs on a different scale. In Germany, people may not expect you to speak their language or may ask you where to find something in the supermarket because they assume you work there, but they do not call the police on you for no reason. There are indeed differences between Germany's regions. Much like the U.S. South, Germany's eastern part is not a happy place, but Black people are not a common sight there.

People in the eastern part of Germany have so many issues; being racist is just the most obvious one and based on natural behavior. Eastern Germans still struggle with the systemic change that happened merely thirty years ago and shook them to the core. They are looking for their place in a world that changed overnight. That does not make the racism any better, nor is it an excuse, but I understand. It does not affect the system, not in the slightest. If you're a minority and move there, you know the deal. You will be one of the few, and people will hate you, but you don't live in fear for your life. The police won't shoot you for no reason.

If you are White and from West Germany, people will also hate you, they will just show their hatred a bit differently, and it takes a little more effort to recognize it. Still, Germany does not have the destructive kind of racism that you find in the U.S., the type that hit me in the face when we moved to the NY metro area. First, I noticed it on radio and TV, where Black people openly talked about racism in their everyday lives. Since I was new to the country, I had not experienced much racial negativity. That honeymoon period changed after a few years when my neighbor called the cops because I complained about her barking dog, claiming that I had threatened her.

The incessant barking did not bother us too much until we had a baby. As any new parent fighting to get their little one to sleep knows, sometimes the tiniest sound wakes them up. Then you must start over, rocking and calming, trying to get them to sleep, and your neighbor's constantly barking dog is not helpful. My wife and I even heard them lock the dog in a room because its barking must have annoyed them too. Finally, one Sunday morning, I realized it had to stop and rang the neighbor's doorbell. Our hallways were narrow, so I did what every man would do when a woman opens the door: I stepped a few feet back to avoid any appearance of intruding on her personal space. There I was, talking about my newborn baby and asking her to better manage her dog from seven feet away.

Once she ran out of arguments (which took two minutes), she shifted gears and accused me of threatening her. Sorry, what? I waved her off and walked back to my apartment. My wife knew the lady and called it: "I bet this entitled lady will complain about this, mark my words." ("Entitled" and "lady" were not the words she actually used; my wife studied in Jamaica Queens at St. John's and was a Red Storm ball player. You might know what that means about her language when she's mad!). Sure enough, a police officer rang our doorbell less than thirty minutes later. There we were, my wife, with our still-awake son in her arms, and me, explaining to the increasingly embarrassed cop what had happened. "Don't deal with these types of people yourself. Call us, and we'll do it for you," he said after a few minutes of conversation. There it was; I had met racism made in the U.S. in its 2015 form, live and in color.

That interaction still makes me angry, but it does not shake me at my core. I complained to the building management, and they apologized. They also referenced "known behavior" and "multiple occasions" in their response to me. That friendly neighbor eventually moved out – to the delight of an entire building of diverse international citizens and ex-pats.

Aside from the barking dog incident, I have not experienced rampant racism in the U.S. Does the occasional grandma think I work at the local Whole Foods when I'm shopping? Sure, but I'm not mad about it. I do not expect a seventy-five-year-old to stop and consider who I am and evaluate how much I spent on my clothing. That kind of approach to life would drive me nuts. Not everything is rooted in racism. Sometimes people are just ignorant – period.

The police have stopped me a few times, though. After all, I learned to drive in Germany, and that comes with a level of impatience and speed not always appreciated in the U.S. (I miss the Autobahn!). None of those interactions revealed anything that made me think prejudice influenced the situation – not in New Jersey, New York, or Detroit. Once, I shared funny moments with a police officer near the Jersey-side of the Lincoln Tunnel when a driver from Texas was obviously overwhelmed and super stressed by the traffic-jammed moment. He screamed and motioned signals in my direction, leading me to believe he did not want to invite me over for Sunday dinner at his house back in cowboy-hat country. A cop observed the interaction and knocked at my window, saying, "I would've understood if you'd gotten out and slapped this guy once or twice. He certainly had it coming."

"Sure, but our nice chat here would have gone very differently, wouldn't it?" I replied.

"You got a point there. Have a good day."

"You, too, sir."

We both continued our day with a laugh about a guy from Texas and the entire situation.

My experiences of racism in the U.S. do not match those I hear and see on radio or TV. However, some of the discrimination I see in the media reminds me of a friend's young brother, who was kicked off a soccer team in Hamburg. He and his two friends were the only Black kids on a team full of talented players, and the coach booted all three of them. My friend's brother, Armah, complained to me about how racist this was; he wanted something done about it. Well, I knew Armah a little, so I asked a few questions about what had happened. It turns out the three Black players were the most talented guys on the team. The coach had told them this several times, but he also told them they needed to take the sport seriously or they would lose their spots – the team was popular, with a long waitlist. The coach went after the Black, talented players harder than he did the others because he was frustrated with their behavior. They seldom came well-rested to early Saturday or Sunday games because they would participate in Hamburg's lively club scene the night before. They also missed training sessions and had bad attitudes, so it was easy to understand why this tough-love coach had no time for their shenanigans. He'd eventually had enough of his three best players and kicked them off the team "until they came to their senses."

This story reminds me that our bad behavior often triggers the adverse reactions we face. If I am aggressive when I deal with a police officer, I will face aggression. If I am impolite with shop owners or neighbors, I will face reactions that match my own.

The shame is that those situations muddy the waters for all the real incidents. The boss who fired me may not have been a racist; maybe I just did not do my job well. Crying wolf about everything makes it tough to hear genuine screams. And there are plenty of those.

Racism is real, and I do not deny that, not even a little. How could I? I have seen and experienced it brutally. Racism is here in 2021 and happens every day. Waiting in Starbucks while being Black. Moving into your apartment while being Black. Walking around campus at Yale while being Black. Touring a campus while being Native American is a similar offense, as is doing anything with a Latino background. Being Asian American became a capital offence during the Covid pandemic.

George Zimmerman shot Trayvon Martin in 2012. A police officer choked Eric Garner to death in 2014. Freddie Gray died in police custody in 2015. Two policemen shot Stephon Clark in 2018. And police smothered George Floyd in 2020. Those are just five of the more than twenty Black people killed in a way that I cannot describe as anything else but murder. Racism is alive and as severe a problem as ever.

I cannot breathe, but my situation is better than ever. When I tried my best, I got every job I applied for in the U.S. and Germany. For example, a couple of years ago, I was in the running for a Chief Marketing Officer (CMO) position at a New York software company. I know why I did not get the job – the salary was around two hundred and fifty thousand dollars a year plus good benefits. During the first interview, I asked why they even invited me, a customer success professional, to interview when they needed a CMO. But they asked me back. I had sessions with the Chief Executive Officer (CEO) and met the marketing team and the position's would-be peers.

I was unsure I wanted the job due to several personal reasons, and I told the firm all of them. I was painfully honest about who they would get if they hired me. Yes, I would be a dedicated employee, but it would come at a price – one that wasn't just money. I told them I had to stay connected with Europe because my family and friends are there – travel to Europe was a must. I also told them that I could not start work at nine in the morning because I had to take my son to daycare. "No problem," they said.

When I got the news that I would not get the job, I was surprised and initially angry. I had decided I wanted the position during the interview process because it sounded like a terrific opportunity. My wife also told me that we would make it work as a family, even though her career was taking off. I didn't get the job because I wasn't fully invested in the work – it wasn't based on racial discrimination at all. Damn, that would have been a nice and easy excuse.

Do I think this is the case for every non-White person in the U.S. when they do not get the job they want? No. Do I believe some people don't want to give a Black person or someone with a Latin-American background a job? Absolutely.

When I had my agency in Germany, I once hired a Black guy from Angola who showed up in a cow suit for his interview – yes, you read that right. The suit was made from actual cow skin, right down to its black and brown patches. Sebastiao's German wasn't perfect, and he needed a lot of work, but I hired him because he had the audacity to show up in that outfit, and he had one of the brightest personalities I've ever seen. Anyone who spoke to this man for more than a minute was fond of him at once. I don't suggest everyone does that, but he won me over because of his personality and his can-do attitude. Also, the name of our agency was "Panthertainment."

Although he was a diamond in the rough who needed a lot of Major Payne drill-sergeant shaping, he became one of the most innovative and creative artist and event management people in Germany. He no longer has the cow suit, though – what a shame.

We Black people must be who we are and proudly so, just like Sebastiao in his unique suit. We must be open and make the people around us deal with who we are. We must also own the seat on the other side of the table and come through for our peers, as I did for Sebastiao.

However, pushy confrontations will not work. It is true that there are plenty of reasons to be upset and challenge the status quo, but we must play the long game. We must be in the position to hire the young Black people who would otherwise be left jobless. We should train and educate our youth and make sure they learn how to play the system until there are enough of us to correct the ship's course from within.

It is difficult to change a tanker's path if you are in a dinghy with paddles trying to push it around. There could be thousands of those dinghies, but they will not change a thing. Having your hand on the tanker's rudder will still take a long time for your actions to take effect, but it will work eventually.

Case in point: Barack Obama, the first Black president of the United States of America. Kamala Harris, who is the first female as well as the first African American and first Asian American vice president of the United States of America.

Many people may think nothing has changed or that Obama activated the White supremacist opposition because they ran to the next polls and voted for his anti-Christ in the form of Trump.

Superficially, this might be true. Objectively, what happened is an efficient and powerful message: that White supremacists are fighting to maintain their position in society. They got their wake-up call that the world around them is changing, and it was oh-so evident in what they saw representing the country for eight years living in the White House. What we keep seeing ever since is White supremacy fighting for dear life. It is now time for all the decent people – White, Brown, Black, yellow, or crisscrossed – to take the final step and change the country from the ground up.

One political office and one managerial job at the time. While doing so, we have to identify the true while-being-Black moments and bring them to light so that there is no denying that it is happening.

On the other side, we have to start taking care of ourselves. This might be a tough conversation to have with each other.

About two years after moving to the U.S., I met with my friend Dominique and one of his buddies in Munich. I told them how annoyed I was with this racism talk on the Hot97 and WBLS radio stations.

Dominique, originally from Denver, CO, and Paul from the Virgin Islands, weren't too happy with my assessment. While Dominique knows my history with racism and that I am not blinded because I may have grown up in an isolated and well-preserved environment, Paul was not so lenient. We ended up having a very emotional discussion for a few hours. Both tried giving me the historical background, explaining the situation we see today is rooted in that history. I did not accept this. A lot of these are just excuses not to take action; none of that ever stopped me. I know what racism is, and I could've used it as my eternal reason not to achieve things and asked myself why I would be mistreated or prejudices kept me down. We have to change our mindset. If we keep accepting our role as victims, then that is all we are ever going to be.

I told them that it was like the people from ISD twenty years back who did not want to take their destiny in their hands, while we demanded our place in society.

There are many reasons why racism still exists today. Some are tough to handle and will demand a seismic shift in society. Police brutality is one of those big topics that won't be solved in the short term. The neighbor that calls the police on me because she deems it an appropriate instrument to get her way is also a tougher topic to tackle. It is White Privilege in its purest form.

However, neither of those will ever change if we don't stop behaving as victims.

We have to stop accepting the victim role in this setup and become smart and calm, utilizing a strategic problem-solving mentality in those situations. Everything else just feeds the other side's narrative.

We also have to stop being upset and aggressive when things happen to us because we will always draw the shorter end of the stick. Bill Marsh tried to teach me that lesson thirty years ago, and it finally resonated: we have to be in control of our emotions, behavior, and mindset. It is all we have. Losing it will always be weaponized against us.

UNDERSTANDING AND CAPTURING RACISM IN THE USA

To understand racism in the USA today and why it is a "bedrock upon which the USA was founded", we have to look back at history. We are staring at a four-hundred-year history in the USA that we want to change. Its fundamental impact on today's society becomes much clearer when one looks at its starting point during the early years of what would become these United States of America.

Blacks were hunted, kidnapped, and shipped to the new world like livestock. This level of inhumane treatment continued for those who made it through the horrors of that journey. This treatment set the basis for a not-so-underlying sentiment that still exists in many heads: Black people are of lesser value as they originate from a lesser--than-White humanity. It is a sentiment so fundamentally corrupt and disrespectful that it is difficult to get it out of both the oppressors' and the oppressed heads.

It is so deeply rooted in today's society that it still prevails in all major and societal institutions. Traditional racism speaks to a core fear: that empowering minorities will ultimately constitute an attack on U.S. values and lifestyle and eventually turn it from renerctocracity into a third-world country. Simplified, with the election of Barack Obama, the same people had a deep-seated fear that this Black president and his Black family would rather focus on having a barbeque on the White House lawn instead of professionally executing his mandate as the 44th President of the United States. A Harvard Law alumni and editor of the Harvard Law Review, Obama was still denied the respect a person with his background deserves. If that man cannot overwhelm the racial precondition of so many, we see how long a way we have ahead of us.

CHANGE MUST COME FROM WITHIN

> *"We people who are darker than blue*
> *Are we gonna stand around this town*
> *And let what others say come true?*
> *We're just good for nothing they all figure*
> *A boyish, grown up, shiftless jigger*
> *Now we can't hardly stand for that*
> *Or is that really where it's at?*
> *We people who are darker than blue*
> *This ain't no time for segregatin'*
> *I'm talking 'bout Brown and yellow too."*
>
> *Curtis Mayfield*
> *We people who are darker than blue*

The harshest thing I need to make clear is that there won't be a White uncle coming who hugs us collective Black people living in the U.S. or anywhere else in the world. This White uncle won't come and apologize or wipe centuries of tears from our faces, nor will he put sage on our wounds – physical or psychological – and make it all go away.

There seems to be an expectation – justified or not – that we are owed something for everything our forefathers and, consequentially, we have endured.

The bad news: help is not coming. No one will ever apologize and award any form of reparations for centuries of oppression, murder, or harassment. Forty acres and a mule aren't waiting for us. That suggestion was supposedly rudely denied in 1865.

The people who would have to pay any sort of reparations are too fond of the riches and lifestyle their ancestors have earned from the back of slavery, and, quite frankly, they still don't quite see the point. They won't surrender their privileges and are ready to fight for them. In fact, the fight already started with the election of Trump (despite that he was not re-elected in 2020). This is not a fight that Black or Brown people have to win alone, but it is one we must start from within. It is a fight that will allow us to play the long-game as much as our opposition.

They started the games centuries ago; it's time for us to adopt their mentality. Physical altercations, rioting, or anything of that nature won't help; it will only harm us. I can appreciate the anger and numbness that repeated killings of Black people by the police or harassment from anyone else can cause in all of us. I myself feel as though I can no longer breathe.

Instead, we have to equip our forces with the same weapons the other side possesses: education, power, and money, which allow us to set forth a strategic plan that anticipates any possible counter-measures from the other side. If they know we are crossing left, we need to show them our hesitation move, let them pass, and go by them on the right. Every move on their side needs to have a counter waiting for them. We need to put ourselves in a position where we take the wheel instead of being shoved in the trunk, waiting, hoping, and pleading that this nightmare will eventually end. We need to strive for education much more than anything else. Educate ourselves and, more importantly, instill education's value in our youth and children.

Malcolm X once stated that he does not think the Black community needed White help. The more I think about it, the more I believe that he was very misunderstood. We need to learn to help ourselves – all the groups facing discrimination today: Black, Brown, women, LGTB, or any other group that, in one way or another, does not fit the "western norms" defined and guarded by White men in their fifties and sixties.

Change can only come from within. We have to start the healing process from within our community instead of waiting for outside help; that only arrives for people who have already paved that path for themselves. My life tells that story.

We need to focus on a few areas to create a change in society from within our communities.

HOLISTIC PROGRAMS FOCUSED ON MORE THAN JUST EDUCATION & PERSPECTIVES

Things usually started to change for me when I was either surrounded by better-educated people (even though I myself struggled in school) or when I sought better education for myself or the family members or people for whom I was responsible. It always has been, still is, and will be even more so the ticket toward a better future.

Great examples are out there already, where members of the community have taken it upon themselves to make sure that youth get a better education. There are those you will never hear about – teachers, people at local youth clubs, uncles, aunties, friends, and others. Then there are those you hear about more – Deion Sanders, Kevin Johnson, Jalen Rose, Sean "Diddy" Combs, and Pitbull are people who have either opened schools themselves or, like Oprah, Chance the Rapper, and Taylor Swift, have all heavily invested in public school systems.

Then, a few take it significantly further than that. David Robinson and his IDEA school program come to mind. A school system that now has forty thousand students and is ramping up to make that one hundred thousand in just a few years.

None of these efforts, however, have been more public than Lebron James' I Promise School. Not only is this the most reported effort ever, but it is also a holistic program he and his foundation installed. Third and fourth graders (for now) attending 'I Promise' School become a part of a program that ensures they have food, clothes, and the right equipment needed to attend classes. It further includes their parents in the efforts to take care of the I Promise students, their kids. It cannot be stressed enough how far Lebron's organization takes it to ensure that their investments are sustainable, hopefully culminating in graduation with a full high school diploma and attending Akron University on a full scholarship.

Looking beyond kids during school time, the program also positively impacts these kids' homes, making it so much more than just a school. Parents are helped in getting their GED and supported with job interviews – an amazing step that will eventually affect the inter-community and the entire city of Akron. I can't wait to see this program's socio-economic impact fifteen to twenty years from now, when thousands of more kids get a proper education beyond high school level.

Russel Westbrook just announced the opening of the 'Russel Westbrook Why Not? Academy' for grades 6-12 in South Los Angeles.

Holistic programs like these are the start to empower poor communities and offer young generations a life perspective beyond anything they could have otherwise achieved.

It is the everyday example we need to give our youth, as is the daily support we provide. Only a few of us have the means of a David Robinson, Russel Westbrook or Lebron James, but we all have the chance to do something to affect change. Invest in youth education through resources or time. Position yourself where you can open a door and help pave a path for those who come behind you. You have to learn and educate yourself. Resist repeating platitudes that get yourself and those around you off the hook. That's not changing anything. We all have bad days, but don't let it create an inconsistent message. We are responsible for our own destiny and improving our situation one step at a time.

Standing idly by leaves room for those busy creating a narrative that cannot be in your – our – interest. We have to become part of the system, the tanker crew, to eventually get to a position where we influence the rudder enough to eventually change the tanker's course. Voting is one of those activities, while participating in public discussions or becoming active participants creates agents of change. Congresswoman Alexandria Ocasio-Cortez is the best instance of this. We don't have to agree with everything she says, but we need to look at her example. Nothing about her says she had a privileged position to take on her path and succeed, but she did because she took it one step at a time.

Sometimes, that's all it takes: us losing the fear of doing something.

Change of Mindset

> *"That invisibility... it starts here (within yourself). We can't wait for the world to feel equal to feel seen... you got to find the tools within yourself to feel visible and to hear your voice."*
> *Michelle Obama, Becoming*

Perspective will also allow young adults to take crucial steps, eventually leading to more economic power. From this, young people can gain a different self-perception that does not include a constant stream of data pointing to a precondition that opens all doors to victimization by the ignorant environment. "Don't believe the hype. You belong!" is what Michelle Obama says shortly after the above quote to several college girls shown in her documentary.

My mum told me something when I was very young, an easy catchphrase that nevertheless changed so much in how I viewed myself: Black is beautiful. I am beautiful. Growing up in the late 1960s and early 1970s, she saw a different dynamic in the Black community – the only one she'd known that showed a proud and strong group of people. She always wanted me to have the same attitude and therefore made sure I would meet the Bill Marshes of the world who supported her message. Growing up that way, it was clear that she did not allow my being involved in daily fights and struggles where I heard racists call me the worst things or try to beat me up because it was beat-the-nigger-day again to be my problem. It wasn't about me; I wasn't the lesser person in that dynamic. This shaped an attitude I would keep, even through the insecure years of puberty. I was to become someone and something to be proud of.

'Say it Loud, I'm Black & I'm Proud' –
A song by James Brown from 1968 and also the theme
of the Black Power movement of the 60s and 70s

Our youth today and the Black community as a whole need to adopt the 1970s "Black is beautiful" or James Brown's "I am Black, and I am proud!" mindset to mentally recondition us to be in an equal position with White America. If we don't believe in our self-worth and don't outwardly display it, then how can we expect anyone else to believe this and change their mindset about minorities? While talking much about the Black community, this, of course, is just as true for Latin Americans. While not burdened with the history of slavery, today's Latin Americans are mistreated, mislabeled, and looked down upon in a no better way than the Black community. It may even be worse, as their influence on American and global pop culture is nowhere near comparable to the likes of Jay-Z, Beyoncé, Lebron James, Rihanna, and the like. No Tiger Woods and Steph Curry. No Barack and Michelle Obama.

And, let's be honest, as long as Latin Americans are disrespected as they are in this country, nothing will change for Afro-Americans either. Or women. Or the LGTB community. Ignorance does not discriminate.

HOW I TURNED IT AROUND FOR MYSELF

Before I want to go into details and make suggestions, I want to stay with my situation for a few more paragraphs. Everything you read on the following pages I did for myself one way or the other. All those points are relatively easy, as it is like a laundry list of items you have to go through until you eventually come out stronger on the other side. However, before you get there, lessons should be learned; these are very personal for each of us, however similar they might be.

For me, it was about my competitive spirit. All those people I've met along the way – from my karate teacher Bill to classmates, their parents, teachers at the Liebfrauenschule (my high school), and others later at my various stops in life. Each and every one of those people had a message for me that I took seriously and made my own.

Bill: Be strong so you can rest in yourself. Don't let anyone and anything harm you, no matter how gratifying lashing out might be.

He was right and still is. Any time I give into the anger – whatever shape or form it presents itself – I later realize that I had made myself look like a fool. Still happens today. Tiny things I can't let go of that make me lash out at times always come back to bite me. While I have become so much more disciplined over the decades, it still takes effort to master it daily. Only a cool mind comes up with the winning play.

My mom: Be Black and be proud. You have nothing to be ashamed of.

I know this deep insight of me. I still look at the White business guy and wish I was more like him. It makes no sense because my entire history and every little experience are what got me to the point where I am today. So why do I catch myself wishing to be different?

This has nothing to do with race; that is another lesson I had to learn. Everyone thinks the grass is greener on the other side, but it never is. We all have our challenges, wishes, and desires. Race might be one of them, but it cannot define you. Be happy with how or who you are. Work so you can become the best version of yourself.

Liebfrauenschule: You belong. You can become anything you want to be if you invest in your education and do the work.

I never quite understood that lesson for the longest time. I heard it but never adopted it as my way of life until much later, when life became so much more challenging and expensive, taking a lot out of me and my resources. But, about fifteen years after leaving school, I started understanding and living the lessons. Getting my degree at the University of Liverpool – which had me jump through many hoops to make it possible – showed me that education is beneficial. Not just that, but it ignited a turbo boost to my life and the opportunities it opened up for me. Soon, I made more in a week than I did in almost two months only a few years prior. While the financial turnaround is nice and attractive, the mental turnaround had the most significant impact. I finally understood that the only limits I had experienced up to this point were those I had set for myself. The feeling of not belonging or having the qualifications: I should've gotten up and reached for those much earlier in life.

The constant feeling of hitting a glass ceiling; I had put that ceiling there myself. No one else did. There, right there in the corner, it said it: Established by Maurice Hofmann in 1990 (or any year in that time). My teenage self put it up, and it took me a lifetime to break it down.

PsyOps: The person in front of you has a history, too. They, too, are driven by their own fears, anger, doubts. All fed by their experience. Learn about their past to predict their future behavior.

My time with PsyOps taught me what I had instinctively known for years, but they gave me the theoretical framework and practical tools to fully manipulate this to my benefit.

> *No, I am not able to convince someone to sign a big check for me or just hand me the keys to their luxury house or car ;o)*

It allowed me to influence a situation and have some emotional control over it. This is one of the tools I use the most and benefit from the most. It also provides me with a realistic understanding of any situation, even as it affects my actions, as described with the lesson learned from my Bill.

Most relevant is my behavior with airport security, TSA, cops anywhere, and the like: we all know they see all the mess in the world and are regularly snapped at or much worse. PsyOps taught me to develop empathy for their situation. What does go through the cop's head when they approach my car? The last person who drove a car like mine… were they dangerous, annoying, or pleasant? The last male they stopped – was it a positive or negative experience? What about the last foreigner, Black person, Black male with a White female? You name the different scenarios, and I ask myself this simple question: how can my behavior calm and ease their fears, pressure, and bad experiences?

The first things sound as easy as they are difficult: be calm, smile, look them in the eyes. Express with every fiber of your body: I mean you no harm, nothing to fear here, I comply with your requests, I have nothing to hide. It's essentially the real-world application of the Jedi Masters telling the stormtroopers: these are not the droids you are looking for.

Quick tip: Don't wave your hand as if you are Obi-Wan Kenobi. That may provide you with a free stormtrooper experience you really don't need.

Eventually, you will see that the entire interaction will go by relatively harmlessly – provided you didn't just break the law in any violent fashion, of course. Even then, complying with their instructions may enable you to get your day in court rather than a trip to the ICU – or worse.

Remember that those you are facing are people, too. Treat them as such, and respect them for it – whether it be the poorest homeless person on the street or the richest guy you've ever met.

Mentors: Think bigger. Look behind all doors. Entire dimensions are behind the horizon that you see today.

To this day, I seek out specialists in their field so they can inspire me to take it a step further. There is always another level to achieve. This has nothing to do with being pragmatic or knowing when investing further resources and energy won't significantly improve a situation. This is about finding more than just solutions. It's like in a video game: you can try to unlock that one door with everything you have or figure out how to get to the next level.

Find the right people in the area you strive for. Don't be shy to ask for help. Be respectful and well prepared when approaching those people, but never be too shy to ask.

Executive photo shooting, Manhattan, NY; 2019

For every question you don't ask, the answer is automatically one hundred percent NO! By asking, you've already immensely improved your odds of getting a "yes."

And if they say no, please listen to exactly what they say no to. "No, I cannot do this at this time." This means there might be a better time for this person to answer your question or respond to your request in a more favorable way. Some of the PsyOps mindset can be found in the book *Getting More* by Stuart Diamond.

Mentors do not only have to be those you seek in business life; you can also choose positive role models, enabling you to set new goals for yourself that are beyond your reach today. Those goals take considerable work and effort for you to achieve, but they should still be something you can obtain in a few years. It is very gratifying when you eventually make it if it takes you forty years to get there, but it also does not allow you to have multiple gratification points along the way.

Things also change, especially goals. Setting smaller and more realistic ones give you a much higher chance of getting you to your destination. It's like the person you ask for directions, and all you get back is, "It's three thousand miles away." Gee, thanks; what about telling me which highway I need to get on first?

Find people who inspire you – either passively (a role model) or actively (a mentor), so you can successfully set the goals and milestones you want to achieve. Each will allow you to look at things from a new perspective and angle. That is a crucial step toward taking the next important one.

Where is the solution to solve racism for me?

When looking at the points above, I realize that almost none have anything to do with race or racism. Looking at this book's title and overall racism theme, this seems to be mighty disappointing. After all, that's the answer I seem to have promised, right? How to deal with racism.

The truth is, the best way I tackled racism was not to think about it. Granted, it took me not being beaten up daily and some growing up on my part, but the hard truth is that once I untied my own shackles and threw away the biggest energy drain or weight holding me back, I started to flourish. It still took a lot of hard work, but that's the same for anyone. And yes, I still face racism in many shapes and forms, but that cannot serve as the eternal excuse not to make it. I had to learn it. Once I did, it enabled me to work on the real challenges that finally got me to where I am today. Had I done it early and better, I could've been in an even more favorable situation now. I wasted a lot of time in fighting a war stacked against me because I was my own and fiercest enemy; because I attacked my own mind.

If you take anything from my experience – for yourself, your children, or anyone else in your life – it's to stop defeating yourself. If you declare any battle as lost before you've begun fighting it, then losing is the only possible outcome.

Or, from someone who always had a singular mindset and an unbending will to succeed no matter the obstacles:

> *"I have nothing in common with [...] people*
> *who blame others for their lack of success. Great*
> *things come from hard work and perseverance.*
> *No excuses."*
> *Kobe Bryant*

Guide: What can you, I, we all do?

In this chapter, I share my ideas and suggestions based on my experience, research, and training. Do not take anything I present below as the only truth; it surely is not. However, it worked for me, so why shouldn't it for you? What is the worst that can happen? That things will improve? You start having the conversation and becoming active one way or the other? That is what I hope for. Take it as a kick-starter for you to think further on what I write about and the statements I make. You can find links for every number and quote in the references section at the end of this book, but do your own research. Educate yourself. Do it for your and your children's sake.

Just know that I made all suggestions to the best of my knowledge and with the best possible outcome for you and yours in mind.

Take this one thing as the only, absolute, and undeniable truth:

Question everything!

KEEP BREATHING.

Breathe in.
Breathe out.
Repeat.

*"Now he has lost his marbles." Well, although that
is a discussion we can have, bear with me for a second.*

Us keeping our breath is a loaded symbol that I will ride for a few paragraphs. As long as we take deep breaths, we stay alive, first of all. We can't change anything if we maneuver ourselves into situations that put us in the line of fire or under oppressors' heavy and ruthless knees. Any one of us who is killed is taken away from our communities, families, children, siblings, and parents. We need you because you are a crucial part of our support system. We cannot lose anyone else. We all are important. We all matter.

You staying alive keeps us from grieving. We do not have the capacity, energy, or drive to be change agents, educators, and role models for our youth and children if we are desperate and frantic. We cannot think straight without you here. Be extra vigilant in your efforts to stay alive. Stay away from any activity that might

I THOUGHT I was Done WITH THIS

bring you under police visors. If you happen to face the police stopping you, this PBS article may help (yes, this is serious):

10 Rules of Survival if Stopped by the Police

1. Be polite and respectful when stopped by the police. Keep your mouth closed.
2. Remember that your goal is to get home safely. If you feel that your rights have been violated, you and your parents have the right to file a formal complaint with your local police authority.
3. Do not, under any circumstance, get into an argument with the police.
4. Always remember that anything you say or do can be used against you in court.
5. Keep your hands in plain sight and make sure the police can always see your hands.
6. Avoid physical contact with the police. No sudden movements and keep hands out of your pockets.
7. Do not run, even if you are afraid of the police.
8. Even if you believe that you are innocent, do not resist arrest.
9. Don't make any statements about the incident until you are able to meet with a lawyer or public defender.
10. Stay calm and remain in control. Watch your words, body language and emotions.

PBS

LEARN WHY U.S. POLICE OFFICERS HAVE MORE IN COMMON WITH SOLDIERS IN AFGHANISTAN THAN COPS IN ENGLAND

> *"Nothing is easier than to denounce the evildoer;*
> *nothing is more difficult than to understand him."*
> *Fyodor Dostoevsky*

Why should you learn about police officers, of all people? Because it might save lives – maybe even yours or that of your sister, brother, partner, or your daughter or son.

The police officer profession is one of the most difficult and dangerous on the planet. This is especially true in the U.S., where an abundance of weapons remains on the streets or in cars or people's homes. This results in the fact that, wherever police officers go, they have to expect armed people (those they have sworn to protect and serve) to threaten them. Even worse, officers are expected to judge and make split decisions when deciding if a situation is dangerous for them, their partners, or anyone else in that situation. They are mistreated, disrespected, and blamed for everything wrong in this country. If one officer misbehaves, all are universally blamed – all while working too many hours for lousy pay. (Sound familiar?)

I am not in the business of looking for excuses for the bad apples or even a faulty police system in the USA. I am neither qualified nor willing to accuse or defend cops.

That being said, it is time we – all those people darker than blue – learned about officers Joe Blue's and Jane Black's daily realities and developed empathy for their mindset. Knowing and understanding this allows us to read the situation and the officer better. We have to be able to anticipate what kind of pressure they are under when they arrive at our scene or situation. After all, two cops were killed every week in 2018, while a firearm of sort kills one officer per week.

Let those numbers sink in for a moment.

Can you relate?

Can you understand why the officer you meet during traffic control might be on edge? The officer may just want to make it home that day, just like you.

You and the officer have a shared responsibility to ensure that no one is killed that day. No, that isn't fair, and no, it should not be this way. Yet, here we are.

Did you know that U.K. officers don't even wear a gun?

Did you know that in the U.K., 0.08 people die per one hundred thousand due to gun violence? It's 4.43 in the U.S. That means that the U.K. would need more than fifty-five years to match the U.S.'s gun-inflicted death rate. By the way, the U.S. is worse than Afghanistan, Iraq, or Lebanon for this. In all those war-stricken countries, fewer people die per one hundred thousand due to gun violence than in the wealthiest country in the free world.

Why do those numbers matter? It shows why police have to behave the way they do and why it isn't just their fault. There is a weapons problem in the U.S., and it threatens everyone.

This is why cops operate like paramilitary forces on U.S. streets as though they are the sandy streets of Afghanistan. American streets have become exactly that: a warzone. And we – just like the cops – have become the victims.

This needs to stop, and your action is required!

WHAT DOES FUBU HAVE TO DO WITH POLITICS?

I might be dating myself here, but do you remember the urban fashion brand FUBU? Do you also remember what it stood for?

FOR US, BY US

While I am not asking you to search your basement for nineties clothes, I implore you to adopt the mindset regarding politics. If you want to stop what seems like the sanctioned killing of our Black men and women on America's streets, then you have to find the people who will make it stop: politicians.

The most powerful weapon you can use is the organized vote and messages. We as a community have to take the responsibility of living in a democracy seriously. Put aside the tinfoil hat for a second and become a mature member of society. You have to take the power you have and make them pay for mistreating you. Don't allow anyone – not the local Alderman/woman, your major, congress representative, nor senator or president – get away with ignoring you. You have to get up and be involved on all levels – and make sure your family, friends, and colleagues do so, too. One angry bee is nothing more than a nuisance, but a swarm is a danger to everyone who stands in their way. Organize your swarm, and make them respect you.

If you don't like the people in public office offered to you, become an active member yourself or find someone you trust enough to occupy a role in your community or even Congress. Changing a seat in Congress does not take a lot. On average, the difference between one candidate winning and the other losing is less than five percent, many even less than one percent.

What do all those numbers mean?

It means your vote counts. You can make a difference, whether the racist next door, next block, or on the other side of town votes. You can bet on it!

Are you sure you want to leave your destiny in a racist's hands? How has that worked out for Black people in the U.S. over the past four hundred years?

Learn about how politics work on all levels. Ensure the people around you also understand the processes behind it. The people currently in power do not want you to become educated and mature voters. Do not allow them to tell you their pretty stories and play you like a puppet. Knowledge is power, and education is might.

See references on the White House website as well as a Wikipedia entry, "Politics of the United States."

NOBODY EVER SAID VOTING WAS EASY

"We used to pick cotton. Now we pick presidents!"
Black voter in an interview in Detroit,
MI, during the 2020 Presidential Election.

Voting isn't easy for Black people. This isn't news at all to many Black people in the U.S. In news speak, it's called "voter suppression." That sounds so much cleaner and does not imply all the nastiness that comes with it. As I write this, Georgia has just seen a new and incredible mind-boggling case of voter suppression. Especially in predominantly Black neighborhoods, incredibly long lines were in front of the voting stations. This is 2020, not 1968. Nothing showcases systemic racism more than keeping Black voters away from the booth and exercising one of the most important civic duties within a democracy: casting a vote.

But what does "voter suppression" mean?

Wikipedia states:

> Voter suppression in the United States concerns allegations about various efforts, legal and illegal, used

to prevent eligible voters from exercising their right to vote.

While this sounds pretty serious, it doesn't necessarily focus on the key story here: the minority vote that specific segments of the political world want to keep from voting – specifically, the Black vote.

> *"Suppression efforts range from the seemingly unobstructive, like voter ID laws and cuts to early voting, to mass purges of voter rolls and systemic disenfranchisement. And long before election cycles even begin, legislators can redraw district lines that determine the weight of your vote. Certain communities are particularly susceptible to suppression and in some cases, outright targeted — people of color, students, the elderly, and people with disabilities."*
> *ACLU*

In other words, Black people, among others, are targeted to make voting for them as hard as possible, while in other areas, voters are literally being brought to the booth to cast their votes.

Knowing this makes it even more resolute that you ensure your votes are cast and counted. Don't let them send you away, telling you the booth is closed. If you got there in time, they have to let you vote.

Make sure you register to vote in time. You can check our status here: **https://www.usa.gov/confirm-voter-registration**

A website, vote.org, provides further instructions and guidance on the voting process. For instance, you can get election reminders, pledge to register if you are too young and want to receive a reminder on your eighteenth birthday, and more.

Yes, it is the right to vote, but it is also your civic duty to do so, no matter how tough the opposition wants to make it. I really don't care which party you vote for, and it isn't my place to suggest either side. However, you need to vote, and you need to ensure you put people in positions of power who will listen to you and do things to help stop racism and any kind of violation of human and civic rights. Whoever the party and candidate that does that is the right one to choose.

Furthermore, something I've seen in the U.S. a lot: don't vote for a party or candidate just because your parents did or because you voted that way the last few times. That makes no sense. Make your candidate and party earn your vote each time on every level. Become a swing voter if that's what it takes to ensure that you, your children, and generations to come have a better future ahead of them than we see today.

Top 10 Tips for Making Your Vote Count

1. Before you show up to vote, contact your local election official to confirm your name is on the registration list. To find out who to contact, consult vote.org. You should be able to find your polling place by checking vote.org/polling-place-locator, but contact your election official if there's any doubt — for example, if you've moved recently.
2. Each state has different voter identification requirements. You should know what is required in your state before you go to vote. You may be asked to show your driver's license or registration card, particularly if you're a first-time voter. If your driver's license doesn't reflect the residence where you registered, bring alternate ID — even mail bearing the right address.
3. Familiarize yourself with the voting device used in your jurisdiction. Vote.org lists the devices used in each precinct, and our "learn how voting systems work, from paper ballots to e-voting" tells you how to avoid errors.
4. Know what time the polls open and close. Consult our poll-closing guide.
5. Know how and when to apply for an absentee ballot if you are not going to be able to get to your polling place on Election Day. Check vote.org/register-to-vote or usa.gov/register-to-vote for state-by-state absentee deadlines.
6. Know your options for early voting.
7. Become acquainted with the candidates and issues on the ballot. You can fill out a sample ballot and bring it with you as a guide to streamline the voting process.

8. Each polling location must post a sign explaining your rights as a voter.
9. If you go to the polls and your name is not on the list, and you believe you are registered to vote in that jurisdiction, ask for a provisional ballot. You should vote in the precinct where you registered, however. If you vote in a different precinct, your provisional ballot may not be counted. Don't be shy about seeking assistance to get to the right precinct.
10. If you feel your rights have been violated, you can file a complaint with your state election officials. Every polling place must be able to provide contact information about where you can file the complaint. You also can contact the non-partisan Voter Alert Line (1-866-MYVOTE1 or 1-866-698-6831) or the Election Assistance Commission (1-866-747-1471).

Derived from the A. Boyle article, "Top 10 tips for making your vote count" from 2004 on nbcnews.com. Updated with current links in 2020 by the author.

Please verify all information as you prepare to vote.

For general information on voting, please consult the below resources for further help:

Vote.org

usa.gov/register-to-vote

Refocus the Narrative!

Next, we need to start resetting our priorities. As it was and still is in my life, the one thing we should search for is inspirational role models challenging our status and making us want to reach for a little bit more. I am not talking about materialistic things, but qualities bearing a much higher value: education and perspective.

If you don't know what you are striving for, then you don't know what you want to become in life. This is an ongoing process that should never stop. However, I appreciate the challenge of maintaining this attitude if you are working multiple jobs a day, seven days a week. I've been there. I had to get up at half-past three in the morning to be at my job an hour later. Nevertheless, you have to.

Here is why.

If you are living in this spirit, you will eventually inspire the people around you. It will shape the dialogue around you and create a narrative in your family and among your friends, colleagues, and community. This can represent the source for change. This group dynamic among my friends helped me aspire for something more and better than a job that started at quarter to five every morning.

Having this mindset will eventually change what you look for, the media you consume, and much more. I am a firm believer in the idea that good things can only come to you if you move. You can't be static for a better life to find you; it never happens that way. You must work harder and smarter, so you can become lucky.

As a minimum, you becoming a living example will make you your children's role model. They need to have a perspective on what they know to strive for. Not everyone can be a rapper or basketball, football, or soccer star. Believe me! If that could work through osmosis, I'd be a Bentley-driving hip-hop mogul right now. Since I am not that, there must be another way to achieve relative wealth. We have to work for it.

It all starts with education. Having the right diplomas and degrees equips your kids to jump at an opportunity when it presents itself. It does not have to be an Ivy League school if you are looking for education. I earned my MBA by forcing myself through an online master's program for fourteen months. That meant working on papers, reading case studies, and participating five days a week – including every weekend – to enable my new career and open previously locked doors.

Success does not happen by accident; it requires hard work. However, on its own, hard work doesn't necessarily mean you will progress. You can work hard all your life, and nothing will ever change. Education and ingenuity are the only ways to change your life's narrative. Be the one to write that story. No one else cares.

EVERYDAY SKILLS AS A BASIS FOR FURTHER EDUCATION

Education starts as a basis in the ability to formulate ideas and communicate those to others. It sounds easy, but it requires training in communicative skills. Show our kids how to read a newspaper. Teach them to read multiple newspapers from different outlets to learn about how various authors create a narrative and play with facts to their advantage. Teach them how to summarize what they have read and get them to argue for both sides. This sharpens their understanding of the information they consume, also allowing them to analyze and keep an open mind. Life isn't math; it's rare that absolutes for right or wrong in the real world exist.

Ensure they also focus on STEM (science, technology, engineering, and math) to be equipped for a challenging future that needs a highly educated workforce. Automating basic jobs is progressing at an ever-increasing level and will result in artificial intelligence removing jobs left and right. Highly repetitive and basic tasks can especially be done more precisely and faster, with fewer to no mistakes at all. The world is changing in that aspect, too. We cannot surrender this field and fall below robots in the job market hierarchy.

If you or your kids have mobile devices, then a ton of free apps are available that allow even the youngest kids to take their first little toddler steps to participate in STEM classes. A list of these apps can be found here: parentmap.com/article/stem-apps-middle-high-school. If you don't have a computer at home or no internet connection, then schools or public libraries can provide free access. If this page does not offer the right content for you, contact me on Twitter or Instagram. I'm happy to share updated lists with you at any time.

I cannot emphasize enough how important it will be for our kids to be educated, thus empowering them to break through glass ceilings. It will be crucial that we lift more and more of our kids into important positions so that the next generation of Sebastiaos (the guy I interviewed in an earlier example) find their own Maurice on the other side of the table who will hire them – not in spite of their attire, but because of their character and potential.

ROLE MODELS AND MENTORSHIPS

Knowledge is passed on from one person to the next. This is as old as humanity itself. As such, we need to ensure we do the same within our communities. We have to share the wealth of knowledge we have within us and use it to support each other. We have to be generous when sharing knowledge and greedy in how much we seek out. My mentors showed me the way to and through the next door. I also looked up to a range of role models, using them as examples to find new ways to improve my situation. Sometimes I even started an imaginary competition to see if I could catch better-educated people than me or those who had more money or a better job. While it can be a reality check, it always fueled me to work that much harder. After all, you have to find your own way to drive yourself to be better and more successful. Once you take the next step, be opportunistic about how you can support people around you. Be aware that you cannot help everyone and that some people have a tendency to pull you down instead of allowing you to lift them up.

MASTER "WHITEFACE" WHILE KEEPING YOUR BLACK IDENTITY

All cultures are different. Black people have more diverse backgrounds than anyone else living in the U.S. This is even more of a reality when you are among White people. You need to learn how to behave around them. This has nothing to do about wearing a mask, changing who you are, or giving up your Black roots.

This has everything to do with understanding how the real-world functions today and what is considered good behavior, manners, and appearance. Let's be real for a second and acknowledge that Black people are not the ones who will dictate how society works in the near future. As such, we must understand the dynamics at work because they will determine our chances in a White-dominated society. The importance level of these tactics exponentially increases with the age of those surrounding you.

Coming from Europe, I've naturally seen people from all over the world and how they migrate to different parts of the continent for very different reasons. If you want to make it as a chef or work in the world of fashion, you go to France. Fashion and design are also reasons you could also go to Italy. Engineers and everyone looking to make it in the high-tech industry might end up in Germany.

However, if you want to learn how to make it in high society, in the world of the top one percent with blue-blooded heritage, then England is the place to go. Those old schools that have educated royalty and politicians from around the world for centuries are still the bleeding edge for the most elusive training. You see children of royalty from the middle east in those schools just as you see them from similar backgrounds in royal families worldwide. Why? Because there is a clearly defined yet not fully outspoken level of expectation for first-rate behavior. Every tiny aspect of lives and human interaction in all of its facets is taught there to tomorrow's rulers. It is very similar in the U.S., where schools like Harvard, Yale, or Princeton still have the smell of "old money" about them that follows their names like a nice baseline does in every major hip-hop song I still listen to from the nineties (*yup, that's the golden age of hip-hop! Don't @ me*).

If we want to play on a higher level in society, we must strive to learn those same lessons. Obviously, most of us cannot afford to send our children to those schools unless they receive a scholarship for some miraculous reason. However, we can all ensure our children are authentic to their heritage while knowing how to navigate and successfully apply behavior rules common in the White world. Again, this is about education, but it is less about academics and more about soft, crucial skills once the other skills open the door for you or your kids.

"Whitefacing" is about being able to get a foot in the door, by mastering a set of behavioral traits do so effortlessly. Still be yourself but do so in a manner that allows you to participate and to progress. It's not at all about hiding, however, but about shining a spotlight on the essential qualities putting you in this situation and making sure your soft skills don't stop you from reaching the next level. Just like in a video game where you picked up that special key several levels ago and didn't know what it was for, these behavioral skills are the keys to success once you made it into the White room.

Use the Whiteface to unlock the next level.

COLIN KAEPERNICK, THE FLAG, AND WHAT IT TELLS YOU

"We cannot use the flag as a blindfold."
Ernie "EJ" Johnson, TNT

This much is clear: we left Colin Kaepernick without support. We still bought NFL tickets, watched their games, switched on shows discussing the NFL, and bought the merchandise supporting the teams. We allowed the other side to change the narrative, to change the topic from the utter and blaring social injustice that happens daily in every city on this planet *(yes, this is not just an American problem. Europe, Germany, I see you hiding there!)* and make it about something as unrelated to the topic of the flag: the stars and stripes.

In his press conference on May 29th, 2020, a rapper called Killer Mike addressed the protests happening all over the U.S. and the outrage about them in the media across the country. Killer Mike talked so eloquently about the flag and how the opposition strategically used it claim that Mr. Kaepernick disrespected it and thus the country and armed forces. It seems to be the go-to-move to bring up the armed forces and those serving the country and fighting for its freedom in every corner of the world. Killer Mike rightfully asked that if the flag was so sacred, how could it be possible for people to wear it on their behinds or on bikinis while behaving in the most derogatory fashion? If flags are such important symbols, he continued to ask, how could it be possible that the Confederate flag was still being shown all over the country, especially in the southern states? If one flag is that important and transports such a strong message, isn't it the same with the other?

I don't see the Nazi flag anywhere whenever I am in Germany. People there distanced themselves from that poisonous past as obviously as possible. I might add that it is illegal in Germany and punishable with prison if you show or use the flag in any context other than educating about the crimes against humanity the Nazi regime conducted over seventy years ago. Why, then, is the Confederate flag still publicly presented in the U.S.? The choice is clear to me: either flags are important, or they aren't.

Stars and stripes… I do have a vastly different relationship to this flag because it represented my birth father's country. Well, more so the idea of my birth father, what I imagined him to be, and how great it would be to live as an American, with everything I dreamed it would be. I idolized this flag and country, even though I knew Black people's complicated history here. It still represented the hope and desire to just belong. I've already described how that eventually worked out, but the way I look at the flag has never changed. Living here, I own a multitude of clothing items displaying the flag, and I am proud to wear it even today, as my fellow Black people are outside demonstrating at the risk of their personal wellbeing.

So, back to Colin Kaepernick's kneeling. He consulted a (White) marine on how to go about this protest and whether he should sit or stand. "Kneel," is what Nate Boyer told him.

It is about respect for the flag, country, and the armed forces' women and men at the most fundamental level. Their fight for American freedom is a fight for American amendments. This is the first:

> *Congress shall make no law respecting an establishment of religion, or prohibiting the free exercise thereof; or abridging the freedom of speech, or of the press; or the right of the people peaceably to assemble, and to petition the Government for a redress of grievances.*
> *Constitution of the United States of America*

Black Lives Matter march, West Village, NY; May/June 2020

Bike riders for Black Lives Matter ride, Manhattan, NY; May/June 2020

WHITE FRAGILITY, OR HOW TO HELP THEM JOIN THE FIGHT

"Make a friend from another race."
Kareem Abdul Jabbar

It is true that reparations won't be waiting for Black people, nor will a White uncle place his arm around us, apologizing and telling us all will be good.

However, these aren't the times of slavery. Your ancestors' White people are no longer out there. I've seen the New York City protests in late May and the crowds marching down Manhattan streets. More friends than foes are among White people, and we have to teach them how to join this fight, our fight, which is just as much theirs. They also feel that things are going terribly wrong but are so hamstrung by the fear to speak their minds, handicapped by the inability to formulate opinions. It is up to us to help them speak out. We need to educate them on the current situation's severity and all its implications for minorities. It's our responsibility to tell them about the fights you had as a kid, that time you didn't get a job, all the times you were scared when you – or even worse, when your friends, relatives, and children – were in contact with the police. Tell them that knowing how to behave around police is survival training and conducting yourself around White people has become an everyday struggle.

They don't know. So teach them. Be patient, especially for older White friends. This is a difficult situation for them because they were taught "not to step in it" all their lives when it comes to speaking out about race. They are White, so no one allows them to talk about race since it is so easy to either sound like a racist or, at the very least, end up with their foot in their mouths.

This, too, has to stop.

"I don't see race," some White people say.

This is terrible. We need White people to see race and stand for it. How else can we get to the point where they can join the fight and relay the message to their colleagues, friends, families, and children? How can we ensure real change happens when even our closest allies are too scared to speak out? We need them to see the daily injustices happening to us and other minorities. Not seeing race means they are also turning a blind eye to the price we pay every day.

I am a huge basketball fan and therefore watch it on NBA TV, TNT, or ESPN. I watch White anchors, hosts, and otherwise eloquent people who look like elephants locked in a porcelain shop. Some – for example, Earnie "EJ" Johnson, who is head and shoulders above everyone else – are incredibly versed in finding the right words. Yet, you can see how this man, a professional speaker and host with more awards than you can count, looks like a slightly out-of-shape ballet dancer doing his routine after an injury. He is still great, but you can see the amount of effort it takes for him to make his points out of the fear of offending anyone. If this guy, as sincere, open-minded, and integrated into Black culture as a White guy can be, has to fight that hard not to "step in it," then things are not looking good for us.

John, Mary, and Bob from around the corner won't feel comfortable watching EJ struggle and others getting nailed to the public cross if they say something stupid. Let's help them get in shape and not be angry if they don't stand the Lutz's verbal pendant each and every time. Let's help them get there and feel secure enough to speak their minds.

That is not where it stops, though. You must become their teacher. Point them to organizations they can support, people to follow on Twitter, websites to visit, or books to read.

Black Lives Matter Mural, Brooklyn, NY; June 2020

RESOURCES

Below is a collection of people and organizations to follow and resources for further education. This is not a complete list, but it will get you started.

ORGANIZATIONS TO FOLLOW

Black Lives Matter – @blklivesmatter
Campaign Zero – @ campaignzero
Color of Change – @colorofchange
Ethel's Club – @ethelsclub
The Leadership Conference – @civilrightsorg
More Than a Vote – @morethanavote
NAACP – @naacp
Reclaim The Block – @reclaimtheblock
Showing up for racial justice – @showingupforracialjustice
United We Dream – @unitedwedream

PEOPLE TO FOLLOW

Alicia Garza – @chasinggarza
Aurora James – @aurorajames

Baratunde Thurston – @baratunde
Brittany Packnett Cunningham – @mspackyetti
Chrissy King – @iamchrissyking
Chrissy Rutherford – @chrissford
Danielle Prescod – @danielleprescod
Ibrahim X. Kendi – @ibramxk
Ijeoma Oluo – @ijeomaoluo
Justin Bridges – @freelancekills
Julee Wilsen – @missjules
Kendrick Sampson – @Kendrick38
Kimberly Drew – @museummammy
Layla F. Saad – @laylafsaad
Nicole Cardoza – @nicolecardoza
Nikki Ogunnaike – @nikkiogun
Patrisse Cullors-Brignac – @osopepatrisse
Shiona Turini – @shionat
Zerlina Maxwell – @zerlinamaxwell
Ziwe Fumudoh – @ziwef

BOOKS

Bad Feminist – Roxane Gay
Between the World and Me – Ta-Nehisi Coates
Black Feminist Thought – Patricia Hill Collins
The Bluest Eye – Toni Morrison
Eloquent Rage: A Black Feminist Discovers Her Superpower – Dr. Brittney Cooper
The Fire Next Time – James Baldwin

Getting More – Stuart Diamond
Good Talk: A Memoir in Conversations – Mira Jacob
Heavy: An American Memoir – Kiese Laymon
How to Be an Antiracist – Ibram X Kendi
I Know Why the Caged Bird Sings – Maya Angelou
I'm Still Here: Black Dignity in a World Made for Whiteness – Austin Channing Brown
Just Mercy – Bryan Stevenson
The New Jim Crow: Mass Incarceration in the Age of Colorblindness – Michelle Alexander
The Next American Revolution: Sustainable Activism for the Twenty-First Century – Grace Lee Boggs
Redefining Realness – Janet Mock
Sister Outsider – Audre Lorde
So You Want to Talk About Race – Ijeoma Oluo
The Source of Self-Regard – Toni Morrison
Stamped from the Beginning: The Definitive History of Racist Ideas in America – Ibram X Kendi
Their Eyes were Watching God – Zora Neale Hurston
This Bridge Called MY back: Writings by Radical Women of Color – Cherrie Moraga
The Warmth of Other Suns – Isabel Wilkerson
White Fragility: Why It's So Hard for White People to Talk About Racism – Robin Diangelo & Michael Eric Dyson
Why Are All the Black Kids Sitting Together in the Cafeteria? - Beverly Daniel Tatum

BLOGS (POSTS)

7 Ways We Know Systemic Racism Is Real: benjerry.com/whats-new/2016/systemic-racism-is-real

From Slavery to Mass Incarceration: benjerry.com/whats-new/2019/08/slavery-to-mass-incarceration

We Stand in Support of H.R. 40 and Reparations for African Americans: benjerry.com/about-us/media-center/reparations-statement

Why Ben & Jerry's Cares About Front End Criminal Justice Reform (And You Should, Too): benjerry.com/whats-new/2019/05/ben-jerrys-criminal-justice

Why Black Lives Matter. benjerry.com/whats-new/2016/why-Black-lives-matter

PODCASTS

Code Switch
Stepping Out of Privilege – The Goop Podcast
Still Processing
tellBlackstories.org

SHOWS AND MOVIES

13th - Ava DuVernay
Becoming – Nadia Hallgren (based on the book by Michelle Obama)
Freedom Riders – Stanley Nelson Jr.

The Watsons go to Birmingham - Kenny Leon (based on the book by Christopher Paul Curtis)
When They See Us – Ava DuVernay

FURTHER RESEARCH

American Civil Liberties Union – aclu.org
Antiracist Resources – antiracistresources.com
Antiracism Resource Document – bit.ly/antiracismresources
Black Lives Matter – Blacklivesmatter.com
Community Justice Exchange's National Bail Fund
Network – communityjusticeexchange.org

WHAT YOU NEED TO KNOW ABOUT VOTING

More Than a Vote - morethanavote.org
usa.gov/register-to-vote
Vote.org

References

- Aclu (2020). *Demand Justice now.* Aclu. https://www.aclu.org/news/civil-liberties/block-the-vote-voter-suppression-in-2020/
- Aizman, N. and Silver, M. (2019). *How the U.S. Compares to Other Countries in Deaths from Gun Violence.* NPR. https://www.npr.org/sections/goatsandsoda/2019/08/05/743579605/how-the-u-s-compares-to-other-countries-in-deaths-from-gun-violence
- Boyle, A. (2004). *Top 10 Tips for Making Your Vote Count.* NBC News. http://www.nbcnews.com/id/6345220/ns/politics-voting_problems/t/top-tips-making-your-vote-count/#.XuGfl0VKiHs
- Brown, K. J. (2020). *12 Books, Movies, and Podcasts You Should Consume to Become a Better Ally to the Black Community.* Well and Good. https://www.wellandgood.com/good-advice/anti-racist-ally-resources
- Constitution Annotated (), Constitution of the United States, First Amendment. https://constitution.congress.gov/constitution/amendment-1/
- Dostoyevsky, F. (n.d.). *Nothing is Easier Than to Denounce the Evildoer; Nothing is More Difficult*

- *than to Understand Him.* Goodreads. https://www.goodreads.com/quotes/209400-nothing-is-easier-than-to-denounce-the-evildoer-nothing-is
- FBI (2019). *FBI Releases 2018 Statistics on Law Enforcement Officers Killed in the Line of Duty.* FBI. https://www.fbi.gov/news/pressrel/press-releases/fbi-releases-2018-statistics-on-law-enforcement-officers-killed-in-the-line-of-duty
- Gates Jr., H. L. (2014). *The Truth Behind "40 Acres and a Mule."* PBS. https://www.pbs.org/wnet/african-americans-many-rivers-to-cross/history/the-truth-behind-40-acres-and-a-mule/
- Gross, T. (2018). *Republican Voter Suppression Efforts are Targeting Minorities, Journalist Says.* NPR. https://www.npr.org/2018/10/23/659784277/republican-voter-suppression-efforts-are-targeting-minorities-journalist-says
- Hill (2016). *10 Best STEM Apps for Middle and High School Students.* ParentMap. https://www.parentmap.com/article/stem-apps-middle-high-school
- Mayfield, C. (1970). *We the People Who are Darker than Blue.* RCA Studios, Chicago.
- Obama, M. (2019). *Becoming.* Crown Publishing. https://becomingmichelleobama.com/
- Templeton, A. R. (n.d.). *Biological Races in Humans.* NCBI. https://www.ncbi.nlm.nh.gov/pmc/articles/PMC3737365/
- Thomas (2019). *Get Home Safely:10 Rules of Survival.* PBS. https://www.pbs.org/Black-culture/connect/talk-back/10_rules_of_survival_if_stopped_by_police/

- USA.gov. *Register to Vote*. USA Government. https://www.usa.gov/register-to-vote
- Vote.org. https://www.vote.org/
- The White House (2021). *State & Local Government*. Whitehouse.gov. https://www.Whitehouse.gov/about-the-White-house/state-local-government/
- Wikipedia (2021). *Brothers Keepers*. Wikipedia.org. https://en.wikipedia.org/wiki/Brothers_Keepers
- Wikipedia (2021). *Politics of the United States*. Wikipedia.org. https://en.wikipedia.org/wiki/Politics_of_the_United_States
- Wikipedia (2021). *Voter Suppression in the United States*. Wikipedia.org. https://en.wikipedia.org/wiki/Voter_suppression_in_the_United_States
- Wikipedia (2021). *Barack Obama, Law Career*. Wikipedia.org https://en.wikipedia.org/wiki/Barack_Obama#Law_career

YOUTUBE VIDEOS

- Anthony Mackie gets passionate about race: https://www.youtube.com/watch?v=b8PGNSa_Irg
- David Webb, "The United States is Not Institutionally Racist." https://www.youtube.com/watch?v=pv7hsiUirUU
- Denzel Washington on race in the U.S. and Hollywood: https://www.youtube.com/watch?v=2tXLCkDOaD4&list=TLPQMDcwNzIwMjAy5FVNRbnt5g&index=2

- Denzel Washington speaks out: "Don't blame the system for Black incarceration; it starts at home." https://www.youtube.com/watch?v=O0dCvQdt5XI
- Lil Wayne, "God knows I've been blessed, but I've never dealt with racism." https://www.youtube.com/watch?v=-PBf_H3z63A
- Morgan Freeman on Black History Month: https://www.youtube.com/watch?v=GeixtYS-P3s
- Morgan Freeman on Baltimore: "It's a Crisis Because Now We See It." https://www.youtube.com/watch?v=gfp-SYs4gnA
- Morgan Freeman on race and his birthday: https://www.youtube.com/watch?v=kOiQgleiRtU
- Why not everyone supports Black History Month: https://www.youtube.com/watch?v=vDs50IVOmEI

Made in the USA
Monee, IL
26 August 2021